The Serpent and the Cross

Rethinking John 3:16

Charles A. Frederico Sr.

DEDICATION

This work is dedicated to Berean Bible Church of Kalispell, Montana (www.bbckalispell.org). Their hunger for the Word of God compels me to dig deep into the text that they might be fed!

Now these were more noble-minded than those in Thessalonica, for they received the word with great eagerness, examining the Scriptures daily to see whether these things were so.
Acts 17:11

www.proclaiminghisexcellencies.com

ISBN-10:0615954367
ISBN-13:978-0615954363

ACKNOWLEDGMENTS

This book was many months in the making. I wish to thank my wife, Karen, for her support and love for me as I share with her what I have learned. My children, Charles, Joshua, Ema, Daniel, Samuel, Miriam, Matteo, Charis, and Wyatt have all supported me in this endeavor with the desire to see more people know the Word of God. My son, Joshua, spent a considerable amount of time on the design of the cover of this work. Thank you, son. I am also thankful to the young man who willingly gave of his time to edit this work. Thank you, Christopher.

The Serpent and the Cross

Why write a book on John 3:16? Is it necessary? As I have been teaching through the Gospel of John, we, myself and the fellowship that I pastor, Berean Bible Church of Kalispell, Mt., have become intimate with the Lord Jesus Christ. We have become especially intimate with His purpose on this earth as it is in regards to the Father's eternal plan, which the Bible calls "the gospel." It has been our delight to breath fresh air again apart from the stale air of the modern gospel, which is really no gospel at all. When I arrived at John 3:16, since I preach expositionally, I had been developing and building the context as best I could. Once having established that, I found that the proper understanding of John 3:16 was very distant from the common use of this profound verse in the majority of churches and ministries who would identify themselves as Bible-believing ministries. It took me four consecutive weeks to develop and explain John 3:16. It was, to say the least, profound for us all.

2

Further, because of the famine of the Word of God in the world and the lack of clarity in particular concerning the doctrines that this verse teaches, I was compelled to attempt to add my voice to those crying out for faithfulness to God via faithfulness to His Word.

This one verse, very often used to demonstrate non-distinct affection from God toward every person on this planet, actually teaches the very opposite. God's love, as demonstrated by the sending of the Son of God, the King Jesus Christ, is a further demonstration of His righteousness. This righteousness is not accepted by the world, but rather hated and suppressed. His love is for that individual who is identified as "the believing one." Instead of a broad love, without distinction or discernment, John 3:16 demonstrates a particular love. It is a love that the rest of John develops in detail. It is a love that is for the Son and His kingdom. It is a love that is for those who were predestined to be heir to the kingdom along with the Son. It is a love for the glory of God's own pleasure and will in the eternal gospel plan that has been, and continues to be, developed throughout history. The pinnacle of this gospel was the coming of the Son Himself to His earth and His subsequent rejection by the world. That love is the greatest of God's righteousness, and it is not available to the world.

God's love motivates all that He does. However, it is not the same for everyone. His love is reserved for those whom He desires. Moreover, no one, no matter how hard they try, can change that fact.

Ultimately, God is love and He loves Himself. This book is dedicated to the reality that God's love was demonstrated in Christ, and is the blessed, and humbling benefit of all those predestined by the will of God to be sons of God, brethren to the Son of God, the Lord Jesus Christ.

The Serpent and the Cross

"For God so loved the world, that He gave His only begotten Son, that whoever believes in Him shall not perish, but have eternal life.

John 3:16

The Serpent and the Cross

Every faithful pastor knows the agony of watching God's people confused about the Word of God. For the man of God, there is a hunger in his heart put there by the Spirit of God to make sure that the people to whom he ministers know and understand God's precious Word. Then there is a confusion, and the faithful pastor is compelled in his conscience to go back to the Word and do what it takes to clear up the confusion. That is my motive here. I have become increasingly aware of the need to bring clarification upon a significant, and popular, text of Scripture that has, like many, been misunderstood and mishandled for decades. John 3:16 is that verse. This verse of Scripture is the foundational verse for many of the ministries that people identify with. For example, in the AWANA Flight 3:16 handbook, the child is encouraged to place his or her name in place of the word "world." Thus little Johnny would then learn the verse in this way: "For God so loved 'Johnny' that He gave His only begotten Son..."

Pastor Jim Scudder Jr, pastor of the influential Quentin Road Bible Baptist Church of Lake Zurich, Illinois, wrote,

> *"Have you ever thought about the implications of the first phrase in John 3:16, "For God so loved the world"? It is difficult for us to fully grasp the significance of this until we realize how many people presently live on our planet. On March 29, 1976, the world population clock counted four billion people, with an increase at the rate of 2.2 births/second. Today, the total population is past seven billion, and it is growing at the rate of 4.5 births/second.*

This is equivalent to 388,800 births/day. Of the seven billion people who call our planet "home," only a small percentage of them – to say one billion would be very generous – know Christ as Savior. That means at least six billion people whom God loves and for whom Jesus died may face an eternity forever separated from God in Hell. That breaks my heart.

Christian, if we don't do our part to reach the lost for Christ, then shame on us. We will have to answer to Almighty God for our indifference. If we want to avoid such a confrontation, then we'd better get busy. Each of us has people in our sphere of influence: neighbors, co-workers, business contacts, and people we sit with on train or plane trips. God has put these people in our paths for a reason. He wants us to tell them how His love caused Him to send His only Son to die and pay for all of their sins. He wants us to tell them that eternal life is theirs if they will accept it by faith in Jesus Christ. He wants to populate Heaven, and we are the instruments He has chosen for the task. God really cares about the world. Do your part to tell others about His love today."[1]

Ask the popular biblical counselor and author, Dr. Paul David Tripp, and he will say,

"What could be so powerfully motivating in the heart of the Father to enable him to crush his Son and find pleasure in his grief? The answer is found in John 3:16 - "For God so loved the world, that he gave his only Son, that whoever believes in him should not perish but have eternal life." God looked at this broken world and the separation between himself and man and was motivated by love. His heart was grieved by sin, and the only solution was to crush his Son, the perfect sacrifice.[2]

In addition to the two examples above would be untold examples from the thousands of churches, ministries, and

---

[1] Jim Scudder Jr., http://www.victoryingrace.org/?s=John+3%3A16 site accessed 1/2/2014

[2] Paul David Tripp, http://paultripp.com/wednesdays-word/posts/advent-the-plan-2013 site accessed 1/2/2014.

households who have been told these very things. One can find this verse, at least the reference, printed on drinking cups at restaurants, bags at clothing stores, and in the end zones at professional football games.

James MacDonald, pastor of Harvest Bible Chapel in the Chicago, Illinois area, has said, "God loves you without exception."[3] The sermon continues as an appeal for people to make the verse "personal" in its meaning and application.

The sad reality is that the promises of the love of God as popularly understood in John 3:16 for the world are not what Jesus meant when He spoke those words 2,000 years ago. The way that so many use John 3:16 today is along the lines of a sympathetic emotionalism that moves God to good feelings toward us. It is a kind of "love" that is best portrayed by a broken-hearted God who is beside Himself with pity for a lost and dying world. Further, that "truth" seeks to motivate the unbelieving masses to return the favor and "trust Jesus." After all, look what God did for them. "Shouldn't you respond in kind toward Him?" We would never say that to an unbeliever, but that is their impression. Some give in and make a decision for Jesus. Others see through it and reject the "gospel."

Based upon the re-examination of this passage, as you will see in the following chapters, this is not the gospel of the kingdom. The teaching that God loves the world in the same way

---

[3] Cited from his sermon entitled, "The Greatest Verse In The Bible," 'Walk In The Word Ministries', http://www.youtube.com/watch?v=rsco4psRJmw accessed 1/23/2014 mark 23:00.

that He loves His Son is not true. The teaching that God loves the world in the same way that He loves His children is not true. The teaching that God loves the world enough to open the kingdom of God to everyone if they would only respond in faith, is not true. The teaching that Jesus Christ being lifted up upon the cross is salvation for those whom the Father has chosen for the Son, and judgment for those who are destined to perish *is* true. The millions who have been told that God loves them and has a wonderful plan for their lives is a sad distortion of the ministry of Jesus Christ. This world is in rebellion against God (Psalm 2:1-3). In fact, the Father is at odds with the world (Psalm 7:12-16). He does not love the world. Rather, He *demonstrates* His love *to* the world!

James wrote,

> *You adulteresses, do you not know that friendship with the world is hostility toward God? Therefore whoever wishes to be a friend of the world makes himself an enemy of God." (James 4:4)*

The loving Apostle John also wrote,

> *Do not love the world nor the things in the world. If anyone loves the world, the love of the Father is not in him. For all that is in the world, the lust of the flesh and the lust of the eyes and the boastful pride of life, is not from the Father, but is from the world." (1 John 2:15–16)*

God is love and when He loves, He is acting within the confines of His impeccable nature. His provision of food, water, and shelter to this dark world over the millennia since its creation is an extensive demonstration of His love (Acts 14:16-17). It is an astounding reality that God's love was not exhausted by our sin. Since love does cover a multitude of sins (1 Peter 4:8), God's love is willing to overlook times of ignorance (Acts 17:30).[4] However, that is not the same as God's love for the world. God's love is in spite of the world, not for it.[5] God hates the sinner and the sin (Psalm 5:5-7; Psalm 7:11).[6] God, by no means, leaves the guilty unpunished (Exodus 34:7). God cannot rejoice at the world, nor pity it. He must judge it (Genesis 6:5). And yet, God is love. God's love is for His elect, His children. God's love is for those whom He has chosen to be given to the Son for eternity as

---

[4] This is another example where God's love is limited. That is, He was willing to overlook times of ignorance, e.g. the times prior to Christ. However, in this age, the final age, God is commanding all men everywhere to repent of their sins and obey the Son (Psalm 2:10-12).

[5] As exampled by God's election of Israel-Deuteronomy 7:7-8.

[6] It is important to clarify the wording here. Psalm 5:6-7 indicates that God hates those who do evil. This is a gasping thought for many to read, especially if you have not been exposed to this Psalm before. However, before it is seen as aiding and abetting hatred, as we know it, consider that God is holy and pure. It is not that He simply is holy and pure, but He Himself is the source of holiness and purity. Moreover, like us, He hates sin, wickedness, and transgression. However, unlike us, His hatred is justified, pure, and without fault. To say that God hates the sinner who habitually practices their sins, like we all do, but particularly those who are incorrigible in the face of righteousness (Psalm 14:1-3), is right only for God and does not allow us to practice what many might think this verse is saying. Remember, Jesus allowed Judas to greet Him with a kiss calling Judas "friend" (Matthew 26:47-50) even as he was filled with Satan himself (John 13:27).

brethren. God's love is particularly for those for whom is the kingdom.[7]

To put this into perspective, there will never be any elect in hell. The converse is true, there will never be any non-elect in heaven. You cannot go from non-elect to elect, nor elect to non-elect. The facts of Scripture are clear, as will be demonstrated on the pages following, that only those who believe possess eternal life and only those who are a gift from the Father to the Son will believe. This is the gospel of Jesus Christ. Thus, the church's evangelism must reflect these realities.

INTRODUCTION TO THE WORLD

"The world lies in the lap of the evil one"(1 John 5:19)

This verse indicates that the entire world is the property, limited as it is, of Satan. He is the evil one and, according to the Lord Jesus Christ, he is a murderer, liar, and destroyer (John 8:44). The fact that the entire world lies in his possession indicates something about the world. Although much could be said about it, one thing towers above the condition of the world: its spiritual darkness. This darkness was proclaimed by Jesus Christ unequivocally later in the chapter. The Lord's teaching is that the entire world can be descriptively summed up by an analogy of light and dark. He said there, "This is the judgment,

---

[7] See Appendix 1

that the Light has come into the world, and men loved the darkness rather than the Light, for their deeds were evil" (John 3:19).

This analogy by the Lord is meant to teach us about the spiritual condition of the world. Jesus said that "men loved the darkness..." That is a statement concerning the condition of the will and heart of every man on the earth at any given time. The Lord's judgment, based upon omniscience, is the same judgment He made in the days of Noah. Sadly, He said there, "Then the Lord saw that the wickedness of man was great on the earth, and that every intent of the thoughts of his heart was only evil continually" (Genesis 6:5) This intense description of the hearts and minds of the men of Noah's day, who were all destroyed in the worldwide flood, is the very same condition of man today. The Lord teaches that the hearts of man are only evil continually. That is, they love darkness far more than they love the light. This love of evil evidences profound spiritual ignorance. The heart and mind of man is completely dark, and thus their behavior is devoid of goodness. This is because such goodness comes only from a correct understanding of the things of the true God, the God of the Bible. Paul wrote of this in Ephesians 4:17-19. In that passage, he wrote that the Gentiles walk in the futility of their minds. That condition is further described as "being darkened in their understanding, excluded from the life of God because of the ignorance that is in them, because of the hardness of their heart." This description is the very same thing that the Lord is saying in John 3:19. The darkness that is there is intense and incorrigible. It cannot be remolded or repaired. The darkness that inhabits the heart of every man is there by an act of the will of man. He doesn't want it any other way. The Lord went on to say, "For everyone who does evil hates the Light, and does not come to the Light for fear that his deeds will be exposed" (John 3:20) Men do not come to the light because if they did, they would have to give up their deeds of darkness, and they love them far too much to do that. Thus, men remain in their darkness.

At one point in the Lord's ministry, a rich young ruler approached the Lord and asked concerning eternal life (Matthew 1916-22).[8] The Lord exposed his motives and lack of love for God and the man went away, supposedly never to have gained the thing he lacked. The Lord told the disciples that although they believe, by the teaching of the Rabbis, that the rich are more favored by God, the fact of the matter is that the rich cannot enter the kingdom. It would be easier to shove a camel through the eyelet of a sewing needle than to see a rich man save himself. The disciples responded, "Then who can be saved?"[9] Jesus' response is staggering. Essentially, the Lord said, "No one." No one can, in and of themselves, enter the kingdom, which is the same as being "saved." Even the best of the men of the world are unable to enter the kingdom of God. It is impossible.

---

[8] Also note that Mark writes that when the man did not see his sin of hypocrisy, Jesus "felt a love for him" and spoke further words to him (Mark 10:21). Thus, the balance of love for the sinner in the face of his sin is only perfect in God Himself. Oh, that God's children would strive after this love!

[9] See Matthew 19:25-26; cf. Mark 10:23-27; Luke 18:18-27.

The impossibility of entering the kingdom is the very predicament that we find in a man named Nicodemus. History indicates to us that Nicodemus was very wealthy, but lost his wealth later in life. But this man had more going for him than the rich young ruler did. He was also a Pharisee, and a ruler of them. Therefore, this man was wealthy and very religious. In the traditions of the Rabbis, if anyone would enter the kingdom of God, it would be a man of Nicodemus' stature. But, what Jesus must teach this teacher of Israel is that he is far from the kingdom and far from God. He is as ignorant of YHWH as the pagans, and in fact more so. Nicodemus must be made aware of God's evaluation of him before he could ever enter the kingdom of the Messiah, the very kingdom he expected to see.

This discussion with Nicodemus is vital to the life of the church in our day. What the Lord taught this man needs to be taught to those who identify themselves as believers and attend churches every Sunday. The reexamination of the conditions of entering the kingdom is in view here. Nicodemus, like many today, believed himself to be the perfect candidate for the kingdom because of his position and his riches. He believed that with all of his religious, Pharisaical duties, he was satisfying God and would one day be rewarded with entrance into the kingdom of God. Further, he believed that he understood all things in the Law. He believed that he was a "guide to the blind" (Romans 2:17-24) and a ruler of the elite righteous of the land. However, that arrogant introspection only confirmed the level of darkness in which he existed. He believed himself to be right, but he was wrong. He believed himself to be able to go toe-to-toe with Jesus, but he was wrong. He believed himself intelligent and wise, but he was a fool. He believed himself to be rich, but he did not know that he was wretchedly poor.

Chapter 1

AN INTRODUCTION TO NICODEMUS

JOHN 3:1-2

There is a legend that this man whom we call "Nicodemus" was also one Nakdimon of Jerusalem. He was one of three of the wealthiest men in Jerusalem, highly philanthropic, and had a very beautiful daughter. According to the Talmud, which is often noted for fanciful writings, this man once prayed for water enough to fill twelve cisterns as well as causing the sun to move back in order to keep a contract that he had signed. After Jerusalem was sacked and destroyed in 70 A.D. by the Roman army, Nicodemus lost his wealth and was subjected to abject poverty. One legend even tells of a rabbi encountering Nicodemus' formerly beautiful daughter on the roadside so famished with hunger that she was picking grains of corn out of the cow dung that lie on the road.[10]

Nicodemus was a celebrated man, as far as history records. However, scripturally, he was a deceived man who was not headed for the kingdom of God. We are introduced to this fact in the first three verses of John 3.

---

[10] Babylonian Talmud, *Kethuboth Folio 66b. Site accessed 12/2/2013* *http://halakhah.com/kethuboth/kethuboth_66.html*

Nicodemus' Approach

It was nighttime, and Jesus and His six disciples were in Jerusalem during the feast of the Passover. The Passover was a month long celebration that combined other biblical and extra-biblical feasts. The Lord had entered the city and came upon the racketeering enterprise of the high priests and the Romans. He saw them selling replacement animals for sacrifice (which the Law never taught to do), taxing others for performing their sacrificial duties, and otherwise blaspheming the Temple and the God of Jerusalem. The entire system was wicked, degrading, and horribly unlike anything that God had taught in the Law.

The entire Temple-market was run by one man: Annas, the high priest. This man was made priest not by lineage but by money and bribery.[11] He was twisted and used the Passover as a time of great money-making. Whether the scales were unjust, or the animals were fraudulently identified as "unacceptable" for worship, every transaction that occurred in Jerusalem during the time of the Passover eventually found its way into Annas' pocket. He was shrewd, evil, and could be likened to a Mafia mob-boss rather than a man of God.

Working in tandem with Annas were the Pharisees and the more religiously liberal Sadducees, both ruling classes and

---

[11] Alfred Edersheim, *The Temple, Its Ministry and Services as They Were at the Time of Jesus Christ.* (Bellingham, WA: Logos Bible Software, 2003), 94.

religious leaders in Jerusalem. Although both parties were at odds, they were wealthy and influential. Of these, the Pharisees were especially singled out in the gospels as the enemies of Christ. It was the Pharisees who sought to kill him in John 5:15-18[12] and who eventually succeeded after convincing the crowd that Jesus was an enemy.

In order to even become a Pharisee, one must attain to it through difficult adherence to the letter of the Law as interpreted by the Pharisees One would also have to purchase the right to become a Pharisee, as well as attend their schools. There were about 4-5 levels of structure in the Pharisee's order. The higher you go, the more strict, and ruthless, you must become. This is because you would have to become increasingly convinced of the validity of Pharisaism and its strict adherence to the Law and tradition.

The last stop on the Pharisaic ladder would be the office of "Ruler." This position is that of one who manages and "rules" over the entire order. His responsibilities, presumably, would be substantial and influential. Nicodemus was a ruler of the Jews (John 3:1). For John to tell us that Nicodemus was a ruler of the

---

[12] In the Gospel According to John, the term "Jews," although encompassing every Israelite from every tribe, is isolated to be a direct reference to the Pharisees. We understand this because the priest and Levite were sent to examine John the Baptist one day and it is said, "This is the testimony of John, when the Jews sent to him priests and Levites from Jerusalem to ask him, "Who are you?" (John 1:19). Later, in v. 24, the Apostle John tells us that it was the Pharisees who sent the priests and Levites to John. And so throughout the book of John.

Jews only adds to the intensity of this exchange between Jesus and Nicodemus.

This man came to Jesus at night in order to speak with Him. Most people would assume that Nicodemus did this because of his eagerness to hear from Jesus concerning how to enter the kingdom. Most would consider him a "seeker" and that he is coming by the shadows of night in order to "receive Jesus." However, that is far from what is happening here.

You must remember John's statement to us (and I am glad that he included it) that Nicodemus is a ruler of the Jews. He is a Pharisee of all the Pharisees. We have seen that the Pharisees are the avowed enemy of Christ because Christ's message and person exposed their own hypocrisy, and thus threatened their religious system which maintained their pocketbooks. Nicodemus was the best of the Pharisees, not a seeker. He did not come to Jesus by night in order to seek the kingdom. Rather, he had ulterior motives.

Nicodemus' introduction is all that we need in order to see that the above assertion is true. Nicodemus said, "Rabbi, we know that You have come from God as a teacher; for no one can do these signs that You do unless God is with him."

First of all, notice that Nicodemus did not come on his own. He said to the Lord, "Rabbi, *we* know..." Thus, he is speaking on behalf of the rest of the Pharisees. This indicates a kind of collaboration between Nicodemus and his compatriots. Also, he speaks to Jesus as Rabbi, which means "teacher." Normally, that term is appropriate and respectful. However, that is not how he uses it here. When Nicodemus said that he and those who sent him, the rest of the Pharisees, believe about Him, Jesus had him figured out. Not only did Jesus know Nicodemus' heart (John 2:23-25), but also this introduction told Jesus, and tells us, that Nicodemus is sent with the consent of the other Pharisees. The statement that Nicodemus makes to Jesus is not that of longing desire, but flattery. "Rabbi, we know that…" Speaking to Christ as Rabbi is appropriate, but not when it comes from the lips of a Pharisee. It is then flattery.

Second, notice what is said about Christ from this man: "You have come from God as a teacher." That is true, but that is not good enough. Andrew, Philip, Simon, James, John, and Nathaniel all immediately believed and confessed that Jesus is the Messiah, the Son of God (John 1:29-31). To call Him a mere "teacher" does not reflect a repentant heart and mind illumined by the light of accurate knowledge of Christ. Thus, we know that Nicodemus, and his friends, are still in darkness.

Third, he goes on to admit the reason for this confession: "No one can do these signs that You do unless God is with him." Again, this simply is not good enough. The signs should have indicated to the Pharisees that Jesus is the Messiah since the Messiah would come presenting signs and wonders as proof of His office.[13] But instead, he limply admits that "God is with Him" in half-hearted admission and flattery. True to Pharisaic form,

---

[13] Isaiah 61:1; cf. Luke 4:18 and Matthew 11:1-6.

Nicodemus is attempting to, as we say, "butter Him up." Nicodemus would come to Christ at night in order to have a private conversation with Him, not as a seeker of truth, but to trap Him.[14] This was a clandestine operation meant to expose Jesus and trick Him by flattery.

However, Nicodemus got more than he bargained for.

---

[14] Matt 26:4; Mark 14:1; Luke 22:2

Chapter 2

The Lord's Attack
John 3:3

Before we examine the Lord's teaching to Nicodemus, a word must be said about His method. It is sheer genius. Remember, John told us that Jesus knew the heart and mind of every man He ever encountered in His ministry. Nicodemus, not believing in the deity of Jesus Christ, did not realize this. The Lord, seeing his heart, went straight to the main issue that Nicodemus needs to deal with: the kingdom. Seeing through his ulterior motives, the Lord right away begins to confront Nicodemus' self-righteous, pompous, self-justification with the teaching about the kingdom. We will find that this teaching is nothing new to Christ. It is, in fact, all there in the Old Testament. Thus, the Lord, instead of being exposed, turns and exposes Nicodemus.

I think, however, there is a greater reason beyond this for the Lord's immediate conversation.

As we move along in the gospel according to the Apostle John, there are ever-widening cycles of teaching and of truth. One of those foundational truths of this book, indeed of the Lord's entire ministry, is that of seeking and saving lost sheep. That effort really sums up the entire motivation for the Lord's efforts in every conversation He had and every place He visited.

Who are these sheep that Jesus came to save? According to the apostle, they are those whom "the Father has given to [Christ]" (John 10:29). At its core, this is the identification of the sheep. They inherit eternal life (John 10:28), they always respond to the Lord's voice (v. 27), they know Christ when they hear Him (v. 27), and they follow Christ (v. 27). Ultimately, they will never perish (vv. 28-29).[15] They are the "lost" who are the particular focus of the ministry of the Lord Jesus Christ. These people are illustrated by the Lord in Luke 15 as "sheep," "coins," and a "son." All of which are lost, that is estranged from their real Shepherd, Owner, and home respectively. Those sheep etc... are the focus of the Lord's ministry. He came to seek and to save that which was lost. Matthew records this in this way, "So it is not the will of your Father who is in heaven that one of these little ones perish" (Matthew 18:14). Therefore, the perishing of the sheep, those who are the property of the Father and have been given to the Son, is not an option. Redemption of these sheep defines the entire ministry, indeed entire life, of Christ. To save these people from the judgment of the Father and the Son is the issue. The Apostle Paul wrote, "[we are] looking for the blessed hope and the appearing of the glory of our great God and Savior, Christ

---

[15] As we will see, this is a reference to the ultimate destruction of all who disobey the gospel of Jesus Christ. They will be judged accordingly (2 Thessalonians 1:8-10). This judgment occurs at the throne of the Father who carries out the sentence pronounced upon them by Jesus Himself (Revelation 20:1-15).

Jesus, who gave Himself for us to redeem us from every lawless deed, and to purify for Himself a people for His own possession, zealous for good deeds (Titus 2:14). This is the gospel of God. The redemption of God's people from lawless deeds and to cleanse them.

This is still the concern of the Father and the Son. Today, a proper ministry is one insofar as those ministering understand that the church exists to rescue the lost sheep of God. We are not here to attempt to rescue the goats. That is, we are very concerned that those who belong to God are rescued and kept safe until He returns to get them. Until then, faithful pastors and elders shepherd and lead these sheep to pasture upon the Word of God. The Apostle Paul wrote, "For this reason I endure all things for the sake of those who are chosen, so that they also may obtain the salvation which is in Christ Jesus and with it eternal glory" (2 Timothy 2:10). Paul understood that his ministry is the mirror image of the Lord's. Just as Jesus Christ came to seek after and save the lost men and women who belong to God, so also must we do the same. Paul did all he did for the sake of the elect ("those chosen") so that they may "obtain the salvation which is in Christ Jesus and with it eternal glory." Notice that he called these people the "unsaved elect." That is, those for whom he labored are those who are elect, chosen of God, but are not even saved yet. His is a ministry of calling these people to the Lord by the proclamation of the gospel.

We know that Nicodemus does become a "believer." We see him coming to the dead body of the Lord and taking it down, along with Joseph from Arimathea, and burying the body in Joseph's tomb (John 19:38-40). Eventually, Nicodemus overcame his fear of men[16] and publicly showed allegiance to Christ by his action that day. However, until that time, he was an unbeliever. So, from this instruction from John, we see that the Lord knows that Nicodemus is a sheep and needed to hear the words from the Lord that would, in time, generate eternal life in him.

The Lord exposes Nicodemus' lack of understanding of spiritual truth on many levels. In one way or another, the Lord's teaching to this confused man is repeated in the following narrative to the degree that Nicodemus had no more to say. He was exposed. He was confronted with his own spiritual ignorance and was left speechless.

As mentioned before, the Lord begins the entire conversation centered upon the Kingdom of God and continues throughout the narrative. The process by which a person enters this kingdom is birth "from above."[17] This birth, which will be examined soon, is the means of entrance into the kingdom.

---

[16] John 5:44; cf. 7:50-52.

[17] The term "born again" is better translated "born from above." The Greek adverb "ἄνωθεν"is better, and most often, translated "from above." For example, later in the chapter, the word is used to refer to the place from which the Lord came (v. 31). This cannot be translated "He who comes *again* is *again* all." Also, it is used in John 19:11 to refer to the source of authority for Pilate, if Pilate indeed had authority over Jesus to kill Him. He would have to have authority from "above." The normal Greek word for "again" is πάλιν, and is used alongside our word, ἄνωθεν, which in that context means "from the beginning." The idea of

27

But, what is the Kingdom of God? It would seem appropriate to assume that Nicodemus simply did not understand the kingdom correctly. Otherwise, this conversation between him and the Lord would have been much different. Likewise, it would be appropriate to assume that today the very same topic is quite misunderstood as well. Because of the importance of this subject, we must spend considerable time on it.

In an attempt to condense a subject such as this down to a few paragraphs we will need to start with the Lord's teaching throughout His ministry concerning the Kingdom of God. Then we will open up the Old Testament and examine it further from there.

THE NATURE OF THE KINGDOM

From His discussion with Nicodemus, we can begin to see that the kingdom is not primarily centered upon the world as it is now. We know this because the entrance into this kingdom is not based upon physical birth. That indicates that entrance into the kingdom is predicated upon a birth that originates outside of this world. It originates with God. In order to enter the kingdom that Jesus speaks of, a person must be born from God. Modern Evangelicalism is packed full of methods and means to get people born from above. We hand out tracts that invite the sinner to pray the Sinner's Prayer. We have a button on our website that a

---

being "born again" is introduced by Nicodemus in John 3:4 when he entertains, hypothetically, the idea of being born a second time.

person can 'click' in order to indicate that they have received Jesus. Some even coerce people during moments of emotional manipulation, whether by a campfire during a week-long retreat, or during mesmerizing, repetitive musical numbers. However, these means are not only far from the Lord's method of "winning the lost," but they actually represent a theology in direct opposition to our narrative about Nicodemus.

John has already told us how a person is born from above. In chapter 1 verses 12-13, he introduces us to his concept which he will revisit over and over again. In that passage he wrote, "But as many as received Him, to them He gave the right to become children of God, even to those who believe in His name, who were born, not of blood nor of the will of the flesh nor of the will of man, but of God." That is it. That verse clearly indicates how to be born from above. It must be an act of the will of God. Salvation starts and ends with that fact. Anything more than that and you don't have true regeneration. A person must be "born" from above by God's doing-His calling, convicting, and re-creating. Those things are begun and completed by God, and not man.

If a man is born from above, he then enters a kingdom. This kingdom is the Kingdom of Jesus Christ. The word for "kingdom" is used about 125 times in the gospels. Not every usage refers to Christ's kingdom, but most do. Therefore, there is ample information for us to gather in order to understand this kingdom from Christ's earthly ministry alone. The following are some descriptions given by our Lord concerning this kingdom:

The Kingdom of God is only available to those who are children (Matthew 19:12)

Jesus said, "Truly I say to you, unless you are converted and become like children, you will not enter the kingdom of heaven" (Matthew 18:3). I start here because of the importance of this statement. Many times, we approach this statement without a true sense of the immense meaning behind it. Jesus said that only those who are children enter the kingdom at all. Why? Is it because infants who die go there? Although it is apparent that the Scripture teaches that infants who die do enter heaven immediately, that is not the purpose of this statement. Is it because we have to become "child-like" in order to enter the kingdom? Although, in one sense, this is true, this isn't the meaning of this verse. Yes, children are helpless, and contribute little to society and culture. However, that general reality does not interpret this verse. What did the Lord mean by this? It is the same as what we are told in John 1:12-13, as we saw above. The Apostle John summarizes the entire work of God in this statement, and that is to make children out of men. God must give the right to become *children*. This kind of child, the kind which enters the kingdom, is such only by the will of God the Father. A child in the sense of the earthly, physically-born infant, is not in view as those who inherit the kingdom. This child is such by the miraculous work of God giving the right to become a child of God to a sinner. Or, in earthly terms, they "born" of God. Therefore, entrance into this kingdom depends upon the fact that only those whom God has authorized to be children of God are then able to inherit the kingdom.

The Kingdom of God was prepared before the foundation of the world

Jesus said, "Then the King will say to those on His right, 'Come, you who are blessed of My Father, inherit the kingdom prepared for you from the foundation of the world" (Matthew 25:34). When Jesus Christ comes back to judge the world, He will distinguish between "goats" and "sheep." That act will result in some going to the Lake of Fire and some entering the Kingdom of God. Those who enter that kingdom will understand that it has been waiting for them since the foundation of the world. That is, since God created the world, there has been a kingdom that has been prepared and waiting for the children of God, those blessed of the Father. Therefore, we must understand that the kingdom is not simply cultural, temporal, nor limited to our society. It transcends all those things, and yet, as we will see, it includes all those things. This particular fact is crucial to a right understanding of the Kingdom of God.

The Kingdom of God is coming to the earth

"So you also, when you see these things happening, recognize that the kingdom of God is near" (Luke 21:31). At the time that all the events of Luke 21:25-26 begin to occur, the believers at that time will be able to look up to the heavens and anticipate the realization of the Kingdom of God upon the earth. This will be a magnificent time for those dear believers who will be battered and worn from rejecting the works of the Antichrist and his people. Their deliverance, as taught to the apostles in this lesson from the Lord, will be a sweet rescue from the tyranny on the planet at that time. It will be at that time that, "The kingdom of the world has become the kingdom of our Lord and of His Christ; and He will reign forever and ever" (Revelation 11:15).

The Kingdom of God includes the restoration of the twelve tribes of Israel

In Matthew 19:28, the Lord taught that the twelve tribes of Jacob (Israel) will enter the kingdom and be judged by the twelve apostles. This is the time when the King will sit upon His glorious throne. This time, known as the Millennium since it will be one thousand years long (Revelation 20:4), is the fulfillment in the Law of Moses of the time when Israel has confessed their iniquities, and those of their fathers, and repented. Leviticus 26:40-42 holds the promise that when Israel repents, then God will bring to them the worldwide promise of the covenants made to Abraham, Isaac, and Jacob. The only time that will happen is when He returns to this earth (Matthew 25:31).

The Kingdom of God belongs to Jesus Christ

This is probably the most significant aspect of the kingdom for our purposes in this discussion with Nicodemus. Jesus said, "...and just as My Father has granted Me a kingdom, I grant you, that you may eat and drink at My table in My kingdom, and you will sit on thrones judging the twelve tribes of Israel" (Luke 22:29-30). Once again, we see that the apostles will sit upon thrones and judge the twelve tribes of Israel (see Revelation 20:4). However, Luke records the Lord's words here as saying that the Father has granted a kingdom to the Son, and that kingdom has been granted to His disciples. But make no mistake, the kingdom belongs to Jesus Christ.

The Kingdom of God, as mentioned above, is the direction in which all history is moving. It is moving toward the assumption of all that exists into the Kingdom of God (Ephesians 1:9-11). Those who offend the Lord will be removed from the kingdom (Matthew 13:41-42) and all who are righteous will enter it, and shine brilliantly forever (Matthew 13:43). That is the end. But, how did it begin? If the kingdom was the Father's, and He gave it to the Son, and the Son bestows it upon His people, then what is the kingdom? Further, how did it begin?

The origin of the Kingdom belonging to God, Christ, and His disciples is not a mystery. We find the origin of it in Psalm 2.

Psalm 2

Although many commentators see Psalm 2 limited to the author, King David, the actual wording of the Psalm far transcends King David. David was a prophet (Acts 2:30) and prophesied concerning the origin of the kingdom.

According to Psalm 2:1-3, the condition of the world is that it feverishly desires to rid itself of God and His Anointed. This is best illustrated in examples like the Tower of Babel and the betrayal, arrest, and murder of the Lord Jesus Christ. Both are examples of the world's rulers attempting to remove God from the world. However, the impossibility of such a thing causes hilarious laughter from YHWH and His Anointed, Messiah (vv. 4-

5). They both laugh at even the world's attempt to do this. However, God's laughing will turn to fury as He announces that He has installed His King upon Zion, the mountain of YHWH (v. 6). The statement that will be proclaimed to the rebellious world is that God has installed His King upon Zion and there is nothing they will be able to do to stop that. Although man and Satan have worked hard for centuries, they will not be able to stop God's decree.

As you move along in the Psalm, the speaker of the Psalm changes from the writer (vv. 1-2, 4-5), to the rebellious national leaders (v. 3), to the Father (v. 6), to the Son (vv. 7-9), and back to the writer again (vv. 10-12). In vv. 7-9, the Son speaks and announces a conversation that occurred between Himself and the Father in eternity past. The Son is obligated to announce the decree, or a portion of it, which has been made to the Son. This is what was said:

"He said to Me, 'You are My Son,

Today I have begotten You.

'Ask of Me, and I will surely give the nations as Your inheritance,

And the very ends of the earth as Your possession.'"

The Son says that what was said to Him was: 1) He is the Son, the Son of the Father; 2) "Today I have begotten You;" 3) Ask of the Father for the nations and the earth.

"Today I have begotten You" literally translates, "This day I have fathered you." That is always used in the New Testament in reference to the resurrection of the Son.[18] Therefore, the Father says that there is a day when the Son will be "fathered," or "begotten" and the reference is understood as the resurrection from the dead. Thus, the understanding is that by death and resurrection the Son will be raised to new life (Acts 2:24) Insodoing, He will receive the nations and the earth as His. He will, as a Man, in terms of the original creation standard, "rule" (Genesis 1:26) and has, by that condition of the resurrection, become Lord (Acts 2:36; Philippians 2:9-11). But what is interesting is that this arrangement is never expressed by means of a covenant, or agreement, or legal arrangement.[19] It was simply the Father deciding to do this for the Son. In fact, the verb in verse eight, "Ask," is a command in the original language. It is the verb that means to "ask," or "request," or even "demand." The sense here must be to make request, since one can hardly see the Father commanding the Son to demand something of Him. The Father commanded the Son to request the nations and the earth as His inheritance. Again, this was done before the foundation of the world, as we saw before. The church has been mandated to go throughout the world and make disciples of all the nations (Matthew 28:19). According to Psalm 2, God the Father had a

---

[18] See Acts 13:33; Hebrews 1:5; 5:5
[19] See Appendix 2.

plan to give the nations[20] of the world to the Son . The nations are made up of people. These people, which God Himself would create, are "gifts," as it were to the Son from the Father. Gifts for which the Father instructed the Son ask.[21] This is the kingdom that the Father gives to the Son (Daniel 7:9-14). This is the kingdom that children of God will inherit as well. Of this truth, Paul wrote in Ephesians 1:11 "...also we have obtained an inheritance, having been predestined according to His purpose who works all things after *the counsel of His will*..." (emphasis mine).

As we make our way back to Nicodemus, we have to realize that Nicodemus should have known all of this. It was in the Hebrew Scriptures all along, but he did not understand it. Sadly, many don't understand it yet today in the church!

However, Nicodemus' comprehension of the Kingdom of God would have been the same as any other Jew of the day. He would believe that only Israelites would inherit the kingdom and claim it as theirs. Some Gentiles may enter in, but only if they become faithful Jews by proselytism. The rest of the world, would then be judged as wretched sinners. Thus, with that kind of attitude, Nicodemus, as well as all the leaders of the nation, would have been very satisfied with their attainment as Jews and their rightful inheritance of the kingdom. Their attitude is made

---

[20] Or, "Peoples" (גּוֹיִם).
[21] See John 6:37, 39; 17:2, 24

plain in John 7:49 when the Pharisees saw themselves as righteous, and everyone else "accursed of the Law."

The Lord comes to that kind of thinking and states, "Truly, Truly, I say to you, unless one is born from above he cannot see the kingdom of God." When the Lord said "Truly, truly" He was using a common phrase that meant "What I am about to say is an absolute statement of fact." If Nicodemus recognized Jesus as a Rabbi, then Nicodemus would have to listen to what He is saying. Instead of being self-justified in his attitude about God, the Kingdom, and himself, he must accomplish the impossible: birth himself from above.

Jesus' goal for Nicodemus is to enter the kingdom. Entrance into this kingdom translates into entering into eternal life. It is the inheritance of all that we have identified above. Entrance can never be revoked.

The only means of entering the kingdom is through birth from above. A person cannot work for it, earn it, beg for it, or do a moral makeover. He must be born from above, and what that entails is up to God. A person is limited by his own abilities. He cannot birth himself from above any more than he could birth himself physically. His limitations are permanent, and severe. So then, how can a person motivate God to make him born from above? He can't. God does not respond to persons. He does not respond to the righteousness of man in order to birth him. The very fact that a person would call upon the name of the Lord demonstrates God's own working to begin with. God, of His own will and His own decision, based upon those whom He has given to the Son, re-creates a sinner into a son of God. Nothing but His own will can motivate God to do this.[22]

These are some inherent realities that are facing Nicodemus squarely in the face. All of a sudden, this man who seemed to be the best candidate for the kingdom is not even entering in since he is obviously not born from above.

---

[22] Just for the sake of clarity, it must be understood that if a person does call upon the name of the Lord (Romans 10:12) he will be saved. There is no question that a man must believe (Mark 1:15). There is no question that salvation is announced to the entire world. As Peter said, "Opening his mouth, Peter said: "I most certainly understand *now* that God is not one to show partiality, but in every nation the man who fears Him and does what is right is welcome to Him"" (Acts 10:34-35). However, the reality that God is saving Gentiles as well as Jews for Peter is only indication of God's impartiality and not a statement about the ability of man to save himself. As Luke would say later, "When the Gentiles heard this, they began rejoicing and glorifying the word of the Lord; and as many as had been appointed to eternal life believed" (Acts 13:48). Therefore, whenever you see a man or woman truly "come to the Lord," you can rejoice in God's work in that person in that they were appointed to eternal life.

Chapter 3

THE TEACHER BECOMES THE STUDENT
JOHN 3:4-8

In the last chapter, we discovered that Nicodemus, although prominent among men by means of wealth and stature, was a nobody before God. Although He came to Christ that night in order to trap Him, he soon realized that he was speaking with someone who carried a message that he had never heard. He had known the interpretations of Torah, he had known the Rabbi's traditions, and he had known the Pharisaical customs. But he had never heard a man like Jesus before. Although Nicodemus called Him "Rabbi," this was no ordinary Rabbi. What Jesus was telling him was not at all something he could understand. The darkness that constituted the makeup of his heart was not letting the light of understanding through. That is the condition of everyone. All men are born in spiritual darkness, which is a euphemistic way of saying that they lack understanding of who God is and what He has done. Whether one understands it or not, all of history is moving toward that day when the Kingdom of God will appear on earth. There is coming a day when sin and Satan will be destroyed, and the righteous will enter into the presence of Christ forever. All the promises of the Old and New Testaments will be accomplished without fail. On that day, the entire cosmos will be re-created in perfection and glory as a permanent dwelling place of God and His people. In this discussion with Nicodemus, Jesus attacks Nicodemus' failure to know God. In all of his religion, he does not know God and God does not know him (John 17:3). Jesus works to replace Nicodemus' ignorance with truth by explaining that entrance into His kingdom originates from above, and not within himself.

In this section, we will begin to see the Lord really challenge Nicodemus' understanding of the nature of the kingdom of God.

In verses 4-8 Nicodemus begins to show his ignorance, something the Lord already knew, but Nicodemus did not. Like all of us, unless the Lord Himself opens the eyes of our understanding with His Word, we will never believe that we are sinful before the Lord. Nicodemus continues the dialogue with a statement, or question really, of incredulity. He ignorantly asks "How can a man be born when he is old? He cannot enter a second time into his mother's womb and be born, can he?" Here, Nicodemus entertains the "born again" concept. He asks the Lord how it could be possible if a man would enter a second time into the womb and be born again. This is obviously an absurdity. Thus, it is clear that his question is not a sincere one. He still does not comprehend the teaching of the Old Testament of birth from above.

What is interesting about his question is that it appears that it is actually about himself, and not someone else. We know this because he asks how an "old man" can be born all over again into a new form. Literally, he queries, "How possible (is it) for a man to be begotten again, being an old man?" He is that old man. He is the one who needs rebirth. It would appear by this statement that his heart is being convicted. The Lord, perfectly as usual, opens his mind and heart to the dire situation he finds himself in and the reality of the sham that is his religion. It is a sad situation to find yourself completely empty after so many years of religion. It is not unlike a person who attends a church for years only to find out that all along he is not being told the truth of the Word of God. The incredulity and emptiness is immense. Sadly, however, this happens all too often. Many are raised in the church, baptized in the church (whether infants or adults), married in the church, only to find out, upon further examination against the Word of God that their church actually has not been conducting its ministry accordingly. The leadership is unqualified either because of some unrighteousness, or their homes are not in the order God has designed and demanded of its leadership. The people really do not find themselves compelled to endure much more than devotional-level sermons. There is an overall tone of powerlessness in the church and there does not seem to be a purpose and direction. Such is the case in too many churches in America.

What we are witnessing in Nicodemus is a man whom God is teaching and drawing. In Nicodemus, we can see the hearts and minds of those to whom we speak about Christ. They

are dark, misinformed, ignorant, but often religious about their "faith." However, religiosity is not good enough. John shows us what it looks like when a person is truly being evangelized. He is being drawn to God by the Word. He is being convicted, reproved, and enlightened. As most do, Nicodemus had a high view of himself and his "perfections" and a low view of God and His perfections. And, unless the work of God happens in their hearts, any attempt at evangelizing is simply a conversation.

The Lord's answer to Nicodemus' question is just as stunning as His statements in v.3. The Lord's statement actually is four verses long, but is simple in its comprehension nonetheless. Yet, Nicodemus still asks in v.9, "How can these things be?" I wonder how many people today could comprehend the Lord's words in this section.

Verse 5 is a restatement and amplification of the Lord's words from v. 3. The fact of the matter is that unless one is born from above he cannot enter into the Kingdom of God. A further description is in order and the Lord gives it. To be born from above is to be born of "water and the Spirit." This particular phrase, "water and Spirit," is a direct reference to the New Covenant passage in Ezekiel 36:24-27. Ezekiel wrote, speaking to Israel,

"For I will take you from the nations, gather you from all the lands and bring you into your own land. Then I will sprinkle clean water on you, and you will be clean; I will cleanse you from all your filthiness and from all your idols. Moreover, I will give you a new heart and put a new spirit within you; and I will remove the

heart of stone from your flesh and give you a heart of flesh. I will put My Spirit within you and cause you to walk in My statutes, and you will be careful to observe My ordinances.

Nicodemus should have recognized this. This passage from the prophet Ezekiel was a hopeful one. In it, God promised to take the nation of Israel and cleanse them from their sins and filth by means of "clean water...and the Spirit," which actually refer to the same action. Putting His Spirit within the individuals of Israel would cleanse them as well as purify them for worship, something that the Mosaic Law could never do (Hebrews 7:18-19). This action from God was the indication that God was to visit Israel and receive her to Himself forever. This was the promise of God to His people. Nicodemus, a teacher of the Law (John 3:10), should have concluded this. His ignorance of this reality demonstrated how distant he was from God, His Word, and His kingdom. No wonder the Lord began with His statement about entering the kingdom!

Nicodemus needed cleansing, as we do now. Cleansing is spoken of in the rest of Scripture in a few different ways. The Old Testament indicates that there were rules for the priests to keep so that they would cleanse their bodies before performing their services in the Tabernacle or Temple[23], as well as ritual cleansing for those who are defiled by touching a corpse.[24] This washing was not something that reached into their souls and conscience. However, it certainly was commanded of the Lord and, as such, it was to be obeyed. The act of cleansing was rooted near to the act

---

[23] Exodus 30:18-21; 40:7, 12, 30-33

[24] See Numbers 19; also Deuteronomy 21:1-9

of actual atonement as it was commanded of the leper, the defiled, and for personal hygiene purposes. This use of water in Israel was important for worship.

However, as is clear in the Old Testament, the cleansing was only "skin deep." It could never remove sins. It could never make one holy. Rather, it could only make the priest in the tabernacle, as well as the worshiper, obedient to God's instructions. Yet, their sins were never removed.

This is why there needs to be a *regeneration*. There needs to be a cleansing that reaches past the skin and digs deep to the actual heart and soul of the person. This is something only God can do. Only God can truly cleanse a man of his sins, and only God can give the right to approach Him in worship having a "cleansed conscience."

The rationale for these things comes to us from the writer of Hebrews. After making the case repeatedly in a variety of ways from chapter one to chapter 9, the writer teaches us that the act of cleansing in the Old Testament, although seeming to allow access into the Holy Place, actually did not. The Holy Place, the place where God dwells, is not on earth. It is in heaven. Thus, the water in laver only washed the hands and body of the priests, but did not wash the heart, which God sees (Romans 2:14-16). The writer addresses this fact in Hebrews 9:6-14. Calling upon the audience to understand the passages we just referenced, the writer instructs us that as long as the temporal tabernacle is standing, there is no access to the true tabernacle by man. No amount of gifts and sacrifices will "cleanse" the worshiper thoroughly enough to allow him access into the presence of God. The food, drink, and various washings are only regulations meant to address the body.[25] The blood of bulls and goats and the sprinkling of the heifer[26] could not actually cleanse a person. In contrast, the blood of Jesus Christ, who offered Himself as a perfect sacrifice to God, cleanses the heart, mind, and conscience. This cleanses away the filth of the dead works of the Law from the heart and body of a defiled sinner.

Nicodemus must have been shocked to hear all of this. He knew the passages cited above. He knew the need for washings. In fact, this very issue, external washing, was the hallmark of what it meant to be a Pharisee. Mark tells us in his gospel that the Pharisees prided themselves in that they performed ritualistic washings every time they came home from the market. He writes,

"For the Pharisees and all the Jews do not eat unless they carefully wash their hands, thus observing the traditions of the elders; and when they come from the market place, they do not eat unless they cleanse themselves; and there are many other things which they have received in order to observe, such as the washing of cups and pitchers and copper pots" (Mark 7:3-4).

---

[25] Hebrews 10:9. The writer, in addressing this fact, deals a death blow to the idea that the righteousness of God is accessible through the keeping of the Law. Righteousness only comes from faith, not lawful obedience.

[26] See Numbers 19 as above.

In order to be a Pharisee, you must learn the process of ritualistic cleansing of hands and arms before you could eat. Alfred Edersheim, a Jewish man turned Christian pastor and scholar wrote, "It was suggested by the Sadducees, that 'the Pharisees would by-and-by subject the globe of the sun itself to their purifications.'"[27] That is to say, they were so very zealous for "cleansing" that they would have wanted to extend that aspect of their religion as far and wide as they could.

The Lord also mentioned the "spirit" as well. His mention of the Holy Spirit here is that of the creative work of the Spirit to re-generate a person by His power. It is likely that the words "water and Spirit" are speaking of the same thing: the regenerating act of the Spirit of God. Paul taught us that the effect of the entrance of the Spirit of God into the heart of a person is the "cleansing" of the Spirit. It is the "washing of water" and it is only possible by the entrance of the Spirit of God into a person (Titus 3:5). In order to enter, a person must believe the Word of the Gospel. This gospel, which itself produces faith, as we will see, provides the Spirit of God such that He might "birth" a person into the kingdom of God. The source of this rebirth is not man. It is God. That which comes from the flesh remains from the flesh. That which comes from the Spirit is Spirit. The source of this regeneration is the Spirit. If man could re-birth himself into the kingdom, the product would still be flesh. However, if God, by

---

[27] Alfred Edersheim, *Sketches of Jewish Social Life in the Days of Christ* (Bellingham, WA: Logos Bible Software, 2003), 237.

the Word and the Holy Spirit, births a person, the result is from the Spirit and is thus spiritual.[28]

But, in all of this, Nicodemus is still in the dark. He was amazed at what the Lord was saying. But he certainly did not understand it. How do we know? Because Jesus exposes Nicodemus' amazement in verse 7. Jesus says that these things should not startle a man like him. The focus of his amazement is that Jesus said that a man must be "born from above." That is an amazing statement and, in fact, demonstrates the impossible condition of man. No person has ever had control over his own physical birth. Neither does he have control over his spiritual birth either. The act of prayer, ritual, cleansing, or even religion, cannot birth a person. The sinner's prayer, as wholesome as it sounds, has done more to condemn people than to save them for this very reason. To drive someone to the point of praying "the prayer" is more for the person "sharing the gospel" (or, rather, selling it) than it is for the sinner. Although the gospel calls upon the world to believe in Christ, the fact of the matter is it cannot. It is impossible.

In order to illustrate this, the Lord resorts to the natural world. In verse 8, Jesus said "The wind blows where it wishes and you hear the sound of it, but do not know where it comes from and where it is going; so is everyone who is born of the Spirit." What is the Lord saying? He is saying that God, who

---

[28] "Spiritual" is a term that means "of the Spirit." That is, if someone is "spiritual" he is someone who walks by the Spirit. This is not referring to someone who appears to mystically be living on a higher plane than the rest of us. A spiritual person is one born of the Spirit and walking by that same Spirit – see Galatians 5:16-6:1

controls the wind, also controls regeneration. We, as humans, can't even tell where the wind is coming from nor where it is headed. It is not in us. Our powers are limited and severely so. In fact, the Lord would say later in the gospel of John, "Truly, truly, I say to you, everyone who commits sin is the slave of sin" (John 8:34). That is, the will of the one committing sin is bound to sin as a master. They do not have a free will, a desire removed from encumbrances. It is depraved, wicked, and loves it that way. It does not want righteousness and only craves what is unrighteous. In comparison, salvation is like the wind that blows. Being born from above comes and goes and a man has no knowledge of it, nor any power over it. The person who becomes "born of the Spirit" is that man who hears the sound of the wind, and feels it blowing, but does not know where it came from nor which direction it was headed. Contrast this with those who assert that our own actions will bind God into giving us salvation. Whether it is the Roman Catholic church teaching that participation in the sacraments atones for sins of yesterday, or Jehovah's Witness' teaching that Saturday morning literature distribution promotes you in the kingdom, or the Evangelical promising that God will listen to your prayer if you will "simply recite this prayer after me," they all represent more of a pagan approach to God than one represented in Scripture. Why? Because in these examples, they all know where the wind came from and where it is going. In a sense, it is good business. A sound business does not do things unless it can be tracked and accounted for. Once we see it not working, we do something else.

The kingdom of God and the salvation of sinners are nothing like this. We cannot determine, motivate, nor control the direction of God's sovereign wind, nor should we assume that others can by their prayers. That is not to say that a person is to simply sit blithely by and wait for God to do something. That argument is not substantial. Nicodemus would have to know that although he does not truly initiate salvation, he certainly can call upon the Lord who shows mercy (Romans 9:16). Again, it comes down to the Word preached. It is the seed implanted which is able to save the soul (James 1:21). It is the power of God in order to accomplish all His purposes (Isaiah 55:6-11), which includes the salvation of the sinner. As the writer of Ecclesiastes declared in Ecclesiastes 11:5,

> *Just as you do not know the path of the wind and how bones are formed in the womb of the pregnant woman, so you do not know the activity of God who makes all things.*

Chapter 4

NICODEMUS, THE UNBELIEVER
JOHN 3:9-13

It is the hallmark of man that he assures himself that whatever he has, he both has earned and deserves it. We expect that for which we have labored, and rightfully so. Why start something unless you can finish it? However, it is not this way in the Kingdom of God. That is, our efforts to enter into it are not met with equal results.

The Lord is showing Nicodemus that all of his efforts are useless. He is a Pharisee, a ruler of Pharisees, and he is wealthy. He has all the marks of one who has worked hard, and certainly with his religion he would have expected to receive the results of his labor—the Kingdom of God. The Lord is taking that foundational thinking and shattering it with the hammer of His Word (Jeremiah 23:28-29). He needs to. Nicodemus is His, but is still in darkness. The work to redeem this sinner to Himself demands that this sinner's sense of righteousness be completely dismantled. Since the Lord loved Nicodemus, He cannot leave this man in his confusion. He must address his ignorance and expose it for what it is.

Nicodemus' answer to Jesus' teaching that he must be born from above is filled with incredulity. Remember, Nicodemus called Jesus "Rabbi." He even has admitted that God is with Him. In light of that admission, he is bound by conscience to listen to Him. However, what Jesus is saying is far beyond what Nicodemus has ever heard. Jesus often did that. He often amazed people by His teaching. Why? Not so much because He spoke in such powerful terms never before spoken. Rather, it was because He spoke the Word of God with clarity, unlike the Pharisees and Scribes who muddied the waters terribly by constant reference to themselves, their peers, and extra-biblical authorities. I would have to assert that not much has changed in our day. The church needs men who will follow their Lord. The Church needs men who will preach, teach, and speak the Word of the Lord with such clarity that it is unmistakable what the Word means in any given passage. Although this seems impossible to most, it is nonetheless necessary. God has not given us a Bible that is confusing, dark, or impossible to learn. It is clear, knowable, and verifiable.

Yet, some will ask, "Then why did Nicodemus indicate here that he did not understand what Jesus was saying?" That is a good question and one that the Lord deals with.

Nicodemus asked, "How can these thing be?" This can be translated, "How is it possible that these things happen/become?" Nicodemus is incredulous, stymied concerning the Lord's teaching. The Lord has just introduced to this self-made religionist the idea that not only is he far from the kingdom, but all of his religious efforts have barred him from entrance at all. Whereas Nicodemus thought of himself as capable and accomplished, Jesus says that he is neither, but rather spiritually ignorant. Moreover, Nicodemus' answer demonstrates that He is correct.

Nicodemus' question is an admission that he does not understand how a person can be born from above without any control over any portion of the process. The Lord rebukes this man and pointedly asks, "Are you the teacher of Israel and do not understand these things?" The question is meant to humble Nicodemus and to make him examine his entire paradigm for religion. His spiritual ignorance demonstrated to his weakening conscience that what Jesus is saying to Him is true, and He is accurate in His assessment that Nicodemus simply does not understand these things. Christ's teaching is confusing to him. As we said before, the Lord's Word is clear and does not contain error or convolution. Yet, here is a man, seemingly accomplished and able, who simply does not get it. Why not?

WHERE DOES SPIRITUAL IGNORANCE COME FROM?

Now, Nicodemus shares his condition with many in the world. There are many who *cannot* understand and thus appreciate what the Bible says. Spiritual ignorance is rampant in the world (and the church, I might add). What is the cause of it?

To begin to answer this important question, we must look at Paul's writing in 1 Corinthians 2. Here, drawing from the ministry of the Lord Himself, Paul teaches exactly what the problem is for those who do not understand the Bible and its wisdom.

In verses 1-5, Paul recounts the time when he came to the city of Corinth in order to preach the gospel. His preaching was nothing to speak of. Many of that day would come into town simply to speak and by doing so wow the crowds with oration and wit. The result would be the giving of money and a desire for more. Paul, however, did not come to town in that fashion. He did not come with superior speech, the refined speech of the learned. He came with clear, direct, and obvious (maybe even boring to some) terminology and truth. His was the task of communicating a message, not making one up.

In recounting those early days of ministry in Corinth, he recalls that he was completely dependent upon the Spirit of God in his preaching. This way the faith of those who would believe would not rest upon the wit and cleverness of superior oratory skills, but rather upon the conviction and power-work of the Holy Spirit. That is still the way to preach today. Preaching that relies upon style and wit is not true preaching. Rather, preaching that relies upon the content of the message is.

Why did Paul do this? He understood the condition of spiritual ignorance. Look further at the passage. In verses 6-8, he wrote that he spoke wisdom, profound and Spirit-dependent wisdom, but he reserved it for the mature. The rulers of the age, if they had known or understood the teaching of Christ, would never have consented to the death of Christ. By that verse, Paul teaches us that those Roman authorities who killed Christ did so because they were in a state of spiritual ignorance. Why could they not understand it? They could not understand it because they were not God's people. They did not belong to Him and therefore did not have access to God's wisdom, which is hidden in God. God's wisdom is not accessed by sensory means. You cannot see it, hear it, or taste it. God's wisdom can only be given out by God to a person. The writer of Proverbs wrote, "For the Lord gives wisdom; from His mouth come knowledge and understanding. He stores up sound wisdom for the upright..." (Proverbs 2:6-7). Spiritual truth is not discovered, it is only received. How did Paul and the others receive this information? They received it by the Spirit of God (1 Corinthians 2:10). The Spirit of God took the profound truths that were in God and put them into words, which He gave to the apostle to preach and write. Nevertheless, these words are not words of human wisdom. They are words taught of the Spirit (v. 13). Paul goes on to say that a "natural man does not accept the things of the Spirit of God, for they are foolishness to him; and he cannot understand them, because they are spiritually discerned," (v. 14). This means that for one to understand the things that Paul taught, a person would have to have the Holy Spirit indwelling them. A man who does not have the Spirit, whom Paul labels as a "natural man," *cannot* understand the words given by the Spirit to the apostles and thus written in Scripture. It is not until a person is "in Christ" that the veil of confusion and darkness is taken away (2 Corinthians 3:16).

This veil lay over the heart of Nicodemus. He was darkened by his own foolishness and ignorance. It is the knowledge of Jesus Christ that brings light to the heart. Furthermore, the light is not under the command of anyone but God, in Christ (2 Corinthians 4:1-7).

Jesus would also teach this very reality later in the Gospel of John. Later in His ministry, Jesus had a dialogue with the Jews, the Pharisees, concerning their own spiritual condition. He calls them slaves to sin and not sons of God (John 8:34-36). He knows this because of one thing: how they are responding to His Word. He said, "I know that you are Abraham's descendants; yet you seek to kill Me, because *My word has no place in you*" (John 8:37 emphasis mine). This fact alone accounts for the blindness of the Pharisees. Their understanding of His Words were dependent upon their own proximity to the Father. Their distance from God, in spite of their religious activity, confirmed them in their lack of understanding. They did not understand Jesus' words because they could not hear His Word. It is obvious that this hearing of the Word of Christ is more than simply listening audibly. Rather, it is the condition of unstopped ears and enlightened hearts. Unless one's eyes and ears are opened by God, one will not understand ("hear") God's Word. Jesus went on to say, "He who is of God hears the words of God" (v. 47).[29]

---

[29] This is a very important point, especially when witnessing. Unless their eyes and ears open, they will not understand the Word of God.

The spiritual blindness of all men is critical to understand. There is no one in whom, naturally, there is light. However, in the purpose and plan of God, He can and does enlighten those who are "of God." We see this displayed powerfully in the lives of the two disciples on the road to Emmaus as the Lord opened their minds to understand the Scripture and to recognize the Lord (Luke 24:13-35).

Nicodemus is a man who is unregenerate, blind, and darkened in heart. The evidence for this is that he cannot understand what the Lord was teaching.

In contrast to the spiritual blindness of Nicodemus, an elite religious teacher, we see the clarity of thought and understanding of Jesus and His disciples in vv. 11-13 of John 3. This serves as a contrast in God's plan. These disciples of the Lord were simple, genuine, fishermen. They were not accomplished men of society, nor did they have the wealth of Nicodemus. Worst of all, they were far from his religious standing in the Jewish hierarchy. Yet they understood Christ's teaching. This contrast served to further demonstrate to Nicodemus that he had a problem.

According to Matthew 13:18-23, it is the one who hears and understands the Word of God who proves to be genuinely "saved." Thus, God's work in the heart of those whom He will redeem is that He works in their hearts, like a farmer with the soil, and "tills" it such that the seed takes root and grows. The evidence of this work is that a person understands the Word of God. The other three soils remained in their ignorance. As the prior context indicates, this is the work of God to call those whom He will save and leave the rest in their ignorance (vv. 10-17).

Again, Nicodemus confessed that Jesus was a Rabbi and was from God. Not only is this Rabbi speaking things that he has never heard, but He is also adding insult to injury by telling him that He and the disciples understand these things just fine. The obvious implication is that the wind blew upon these fishermen, but is circumventing this religious leader.

What did the disciples know? The Lord changes to the plural noun which indicates a reference to Himself and the only other ones present, the disciples. At this point, the Lord has six disciples. They have all testified that Jesus is the Messiah, the Son of God. They have understood that, and with minimal conversation. However, Nicodemus, in his astute position, is laboring to even grasp the simplest of Jesus' teaching.

This illustrates a very important element in the Lord's ministry. Only those who are "babes" will receive teaching from God. We understand this because of the Lord's Words in Matthew 11:25-26. The Lord praises the Father saying, "...at that time Jesus said, 'I praise You, Father, Lord of heaven and earth, that You have hidden these things from the wise and intelligent and have revealed them to infants. Yes, Father, for this way was well-pleasing in Your sight.'" This is the will of the Father: only the "poor in spirit" will receive the kingdom (Matthew 5:3). It is the lowly and meek who inherit God. The problem is, we are all proud. However, through the work of God to prepare the soil of the heart to receive the Word of God, we can be humbled and contrite so that we can understand God's truth. Nicodemus is a "wise and intelligent" man. The woman at the well, in John 4, is an example of a "babe" who understands the Lord's teaching. Who is responsible for all of this? Jesus said that the Father was well-pleased to hide truth from some and give it to others.

Nicodemus does not accept the testimony of the informed Lord and His disciples (vv. 11-12). Nicodemus is not willing to do the will of the Father and therefore has truth withheld from him (John 7:17). Yet, the disciples understand that Jesus is the "Son of Man." The Son of Man was the Son of God, Messiah, and the Lamb of God. He is spoken of in the Old Testament in all of these terms. John uses the title "Son of Man" thirteen times in his book showing its significance.

The Messianic title "Son of Man" comes directly from Daniel 7:9-14. In that passage, the vision which is given to Daniel is full of power. The picture is the future when the Ancient of Days (God the Father) sits upon His throne to judge, as well as multiple thrones around Him. He is brilliant and glorious and after His regal entrance, the court sits and the books are opened (v. 10b). Jumping to v. 13, we see that one comes to Him and is presented before Him. It is to this One that a kingdom, and a dominion was given. The peoples of the earth would serve Him and would do so forever! What a glorious picture! Who is this man? He is the Son of Man. He is One who is the Son of God and Son of Man. That is, He is the eternal Son of God dwelling with the Father, but He also became a Man. And it is to this "Man" that the dominion is given. This is what John means when He uses the phrase, "Son of Man." Nicodemus should have realized that he was actually speaking with the Son of Man! He comes from above. He is not of this earth, but Nicodemus is. For Nicodemus simply to say, "We know that...you come from God" is woefully inaccurate and demeaning considering the fact that Jesus actually *is* God.

Chapter 5

THE SERPENT AND THE CROSS
JOHN 3:14-16

We turn our attention now to the heart of the Lord's teaching to Nicodemus, and the heart of John's writing in this section. It concerns the Old Testament historical narrative of the serpents in the desert, and how that event correlates with Jesus Christ. This portion of Scripture has a depth unmatched in its context. The profundity of this teaching by the Lord is immense and deserves deep consideration. We will spend a greater amount of time in this section until the end of the chapter than we did in the previous thirteen verses. We will do a quick overview of this section and then go back and look at it carefully.

It must be remembered throughout this section that the Lord is speaking to Nicodemus. He is not teaching apart from that conversation. This is the heart of that conversation. This is vital because we need to see this section as addressing the religious "perfection" as well as the spiritual ignorance of Nicodemus as discussed above. Thus, John 3:14-21, in a sense, ends the discussion with this religious leader. It would appear, since there is no more indication that Jesus and Nicodemus spoke further, that Nicodemus simply behaved in a manner commensurate with one who is in the presence of God—silence. There is no more to say. There is no more dialogue.

THE SERPENT

Israel is God's nation. God said to them from their beginning that, "I am the Lord your God, who brought you out of the land of Egypt, out of the house of slavery" (Exodus 20:2). They also will be His people for eternity, consisting of the twelve original tribes from Jacob. Although they are God's people, they have not always behaved in a manner consistent with their God. One such example is the event in our narrative in John 3.

Complaining is a sin, it always has been and always will be. Complaining starts in the heart as a discontentment with God's will. It then builds into verbalizing it to others, and then matures into full-blown rebellion. If left unchecked, it will destroy everyone and everything associated with it. That is the situation before us in the desert with God's people in Numbers 21:6-9. This is admittedly a short section. However, the truths here are immense.

Moses wrote:

"The Lord sent fiery serpents among the people and they bit the people, so that many people of Israel died.

So the people came to Moses and said, "We have sinned, because we have spoken against the Lord and you; intercede with the Lord, that He may remove the serpents from us." And Moses interceded for the people.

The Serpent and the Cross

Then the Lord said to Moses, "Make a fiery serpent, and set it on a standard; and it shall come about, that everyone who is bitten, when he looks at it, he will live."

And Moses made a bronze serpent and set it on the standard; and it came about, that if a serpent bit any man, when he looked to the bronze serpent, he lived."

The people have been rescued from the tyranny of Egypt. They have been brought to Mt. Sinai and given God's Law. They have been brought to the edge of the land, which God promised to their father Abraham and sent spies into that land in order to assess the situation (Numbers 13). Twelve spies were sent out and all twelve made it back. However, ten of the twelve had a report of faithlessness and rejection of the promise and plan of God for them. Two spies, Caleb and Moses' assistant, Joshua, attempted to convince the people of the reality that God will give them the land and that they should not listen to bad reports. The bad reports of the stronger inhabitants of the land spread fear throughout the people and they complain and rebel. This pattern of fear, complaint, and rebellion is the mark of the book of Numbers. For their rebellion against the promise of God and His command to take the land, God forced the entire generation of Israelites to remain in the wilderness/desert for 40 years.[30] It

---

[30] Numbers 14:34; Each of the years corresponds to the number of days the spies were in the land. God forced that generation to "bear [their] guilt a year" for each day they were spying. Of course, Joshua and Caleb were allowed to enter the land because of the twelve, they were the only two who were faithful.

was during that 40-year period that the book of Numbers was written.

In the midst of those 40 years, Israel enters the Negev, the southern region of Palestine, and encounters Arad, a Canaanite king (21:1ff.). Israel made a vow to the Lord that if He would deliver them, they will destroy Arad and his people as they were supposed to do (v. 2). God delivered Israel and they destroyed Arad and their people. However, instead of rejoicing, they grew impatient because the long walk that ensued after that. Their complaints were nothing new. It was said before,

"The people spoke against God and Moses, "Why have you brought us up out of Egypt to die in the wilderness? For there is no food and no water, and we loathe this miserable food." (Numbers 21:5)

Can you imagine these people saying this after all that God has provided for them? Or, how about us. Do we complain about God's lack of provision, as we define it, even though He has provided so much care for us in the past? That is why complaining is so horrendous and leads to further rebellion. It must stop. Proverbs states,

"Drive out the scoffer, and contention will go out, even strife and dishonor will cease." (Proverbs 22:10)

This situation with Israel is nothing more than raw complaining. The complaining in which Israel was engaged is the kind of complaining that is from the heart and soul.[31] It is heartfelt and purposeful. It is not a slip of the tongue. These people despised what God had given them to eat, which was a sign of God's care and love for these people. This complaining is from a heart that is filled with discontentment and spite against God, by no means an innocent complaint.

Thus, God sends the serpents in order to severely punish the people, not to scare them into obedience. But, why would God go to such an extreme? Why would God punish with death something as seemingly innocuous as complaining? Was it overkill to do so? A question like this really stems from a similar question: if God is so good, why do so many bad things happen?

Because of the importance of this teaching from our Lord's conversation with Nicodemus, we must take some time and consider an answer to this popular question.

As we will learn from the Lord's latter conversation, all men are doomed to perish. The Apostle Paul wrote,

> "Therefore, just as through one man sin entered into the world, and death through sin, and so death spread to all men, because all sinned" (Romans 5:12)

This is the teaching of the entirety of Scripture. Death has spread to all men (and women) because of the disobedience of one man, Adam. Why? Because, it was to Adam that God had

---

[31] The Hebrew in Numbers 21:5 is, "Our soul has disgust for this wretched food." (וְנַפְשֵׁנוּ קָצָה בַּלֶּחֶם הַקְּלֹקֵל).

given instruction to eat everything freely in the garden, but do not eat of the Tree of the Knowledge of Good and Evil (Genesis 2:15-17). God then said to him, if you do eat of it, you will surely die. Death was promised to Adam if he should ever eat from that tree. He had full access to the Tree of Life already. He had full access to all the glories of the garden. But by the cunning of Satan, and the allurement of Eve, who herself was deceived, he disobeyed and God followed through on His promise. As simplistic as this seems, it is the answer. Many who ask why God "allows" for bad things to happen, as in death, ask in a way that seems to impugn God. It is as if they believe that God is doing evil by His actions. The fact of the matter is that we are the ones who did evil in Adam. Further, we do evil every day. Who has not sinned? Surely, you don't believe that you have never sinned. Earlier in the book, Paul gave the verdict upon all mankind. He wrote, from inspired Scripture:

> *"...as it is written,*
> *There is none righteous, not even one;*
> *There is none who understands,*
> *There is none who seeks for God;*
> *All have turned aside, together they have become useless;*
> *There is none who does good,*
> *There is not even one.*
> *Their throat is an open grave,*
> *With their tongues they keep deceiving,*
> *The poison of asps is under their lips;*
> *Whose mouth is full of cursing and bitterness;*
> *Their feet are swift to shed blood,*
> *Destruction and misery are in their paths,*
> *And the path of peace they have not known.*
> *There is no fear of God before their eyes." (Romans 3:10-*
> *18)*

The verdict by God in these Scriptures does not impugn God, but man. We are the ones who have done no righteousness. We are the ones who do no good. We are the ones who love violence, swearing, and destruction. Ultimately, and most incredibly, there is no fear of God before our eyes. When a person asks why God appears to do evil by carrying out His judgment on mankind, we must respond the way Job did:

"Then Job answered the Lord and said,
Behold, I am insignificant; what can I reply to You?
I lay my hand on my mouth.
Once I have spoken, and I will not answer;
Even twice, and I will add nothing more." (Job 40:3-5)

That is not to say that the death of anyone is the joy of God. It is not.[32] I cannot even imagine the sadness of God at the death of the wicked. However, in that compassion there is also faithfulness. Faithfulness, not to us, but to Himself. Paul also wrote,

If we are faithless, He remains faithful, for He cannot deny Himself. (2 Timothy 2:13)

Since God is righteous, just, and holy, He must be faithful to Himself and remove that which is unholy. He had told Adam that He would do that by death. Therefore, death is the impending doom of everyone. God cannot be partial to anyone.

---

[32] Ezekiel 18:23, 32,; 33:11

Anyone who sins must die. And, since everyone has sinned, death is the conclusion of life for everyone. However, the greatest display of this justice is the death of the Son of God. Let me say it again, the death of the Son is the greatest display of His justice. If someone wants to be angry with God for killing people with serpents, then surely they would be angry with God in the death of His Son!

Let us return to our passage in Numbers 21. There is some history here that we need to understand if we are to continue. In Numbers 11, we find that the rebellion that was the result of complaining was actually instigated by a handful of people who came out of Egypt with the sons of Jacob. They are called "rabble." They are the "mixed multitude" of Exodus 12:38. Whether they were Egyptians or Hebrews is not clear. Regardless, they were not quality people. These people appear to have been the instigators against God and Moses in that they despised God's provision of manna (vv. 6-9).[33] They would have rather rejected their salvation from Egypt and the covenant of Abraham in order to go back to Egypt as slaves. They would have been well-fed slaves (or so they thought), but slaves nonetheless. They would rather have Egypt, a wicked and perverse nation of idolaters, care for their needs than the loving God of the cosmos. It was these rabble who incited the discontentment that led to complaining, which in turn led to rebellion, and ultimately to judgment. That is the pattern, for both them and us.

---

[33] See also Numbers 16:13; 20:3-4.

The righteousness that demands that the scoffer, or complainer, cease is the same righteousness that works to drive that scoffer out. In this case, God is the One driving the scoffers out, the complaining Israelites. How does He do that? Verse six of chapter 21 of Numbers says that God sent "fiery serpents" among the people and those snakes did what snakes do—they bit the people. The people, who were described in the previous verse as speaking against Moses and God, are now faced with their punishment for such scoffing. The snakes fatally bit numbers of people in the Israelite camp. The people then came to Moses and said, "We have sinned, because we have spoken against the Lord and you; intercede with the Lord, that He may remove the serpents from us." They recognized that God had begun to punish them for their sin of complaining, and they then confessed their sin to Moses asking him to intercede on their behalf so that the snakes would be removed.

Moses prayed indeed. After praying, God spoke to Moses and said, "Make a fiery serpent, and set it on a standard; and it shall come about, that everyone who is bitten, when he looks at it, he will live" (v. 8). This is an interesting thing the Lord said. A few observations are in order.

First, Moses prayed as the people instructed him. That would seem apparent by the fact that they asked Moses to pray that the snakes be removed. The assumption is that he did just that because verse 7 says, "And Moses interceded for the people."

Second, even though Moses prayed for the *removal* of the serpents, God did not say, "Okay, I will relent." Instead, He gave some very strange-sounding instructions to Moses. However, as we will see, these instructions evidence a brilliance and wisdom that acts as a backdrop for redemption to come like nothing else.

God's Strange Instructions

Numbers 21:8

Then the Lord said to Moses, "Make a fiery serpent, and set it on a standard; and it shall come about, that everyone who is bitten, when he looks at it, he will live."

Again, Moses did not ask for a serpent on a pole. He was asked to pray for the snakes to be taken out as quickly as they came in. Why? Because, these snakes were infiltrating the camp and fatally biting the inhabitants therein. We would have to assume this included men, women, and children. This was a tremendous devastation. Imagine being out gathering wood in your tunic and sandals. In the brush is a snake that has only one ambition—to bite you. That snake fastens itself to your heel, ankle, or calf. After doing that, it slithers off and you, possibly within minutes, are dead. The assumption is that this was happening on a camp-wide scale and was devastating. It is no wonder that the only possible remedy in the minds of the Israelites is that of removal of the snakes.

Yet, God did not remove the snakes. He could have, but He didn't. Instead, God instructed Moses to fashion either bronze or copper into a mould similar to the snakes that were biting the Israelites. They were "fiery" in color. That is, they were either a reddish color or were shiny. Either way, the serpents stood out. God's instruction to Moses was to replicate that kind of shiny

71

serpent and make it in such a way that it can be fastened to a pole that will elevate the snake high into the air. This way all might be able to see it, or at least look in its general direction.

God told Moses to "make" this serpent. What is the purpose? It is obviously very different from what the Israelites were expecting. The purpose is mentioned in the rest of v. 8. Here God says, "and it shall come about, that everyone who is bitten, when he looks at it, he will live." The purpose is that anyone will be able to look at the serpent Moses created by metallurgy fastened to the pole and once they do that they will not die. But did you notice that they are to do this only *after they were bitten?* God did nothing to prevent them from being bitten. He only promised deliverance from the poison of the snake after being bitten. This is not at all what was asked for. But, the result of God's instructions are the same as they were asking—escape from death.

The Purpose of the Instructions

Why would God do this? Why would God allow someone to feel the pain of the puncture of the fangs, with the subsequent injection of venom, of these serpents? Because God is not concerned about physical death as much as He is about eternal judgment. Think about it: only those who listen to these instructions obey them, and immediately look at the fashioned serpent will live. That would indicate that those people *believe*

72

not only in Moses who told them, but YHWH who instructed Moses. Thus, this obedient faith would rescue them from calamity, the calamity they themselves instigated.

But this raises a question: "These were rebellious, complaining people who did not believe in YHWH to begin with.[34] How is it that they would follow these instructions that were so counterintuitive in the first place?" Think it through: the Israelite would be bitten by a fiery-colored snake, and then they are instructed to turn around and look at a fiery-colored snake on a pole in hopes that they won't die! Nobody, really, in his or her right mind would buy that. That is the point of the entire episode however. It is not in man to behave in this way, especially if God Himself instructs people to do it. There is a rebellion deep in the heart of every person ever born and that rebellion is aimed directly at God. Whether it is the antediluvian world of Noah (Genesis 6:1-5), or the wicked, unbelieving world of Jesus' day (Luke 11:29), or the people among whom the Apostle Paul ministered (Philippians 2:14-15), the world is in rebellion against God and His Son (Psalm 2:1-3). So, to expect the people of Israel to obey God, especially instructions as seemingly ludicrous as that of looking at a replica of something that just bit you, is just too optimistic to say the least.

---

[34] See Numbers 14:11; cf. Psalm 106:24. This actually becomes the main issue. Just like their father Abraham, they needed to believe in YHWH (Genesis 15:6). The fact of the matter is, all their rebellion is the fruit of their unbelief. This is also the main issue addressed in the Lord's ministry. The unbelief of the people Jesus ministered to led to their rebellion against Him.

The Paradox of the Instructions

This paradox is exactly what is needed for God to be glorified. The impossibility of man exhibiting righteousness, especially the most supreme act of righteousness, which is belief in God, is obvious. Not only is it impossible for people to believe in the God of the Bible, but they, in fact, do not want to. Jesus said, "...the Light has come into the world, and men loved the darkness rather than the Light, for their deeds were evil."[35] Thus, it is wrong that, as some have said, God cannot expect from us what we cannot do. God does expect from His creation the very thing for which He created it—His own glory.[36] Jesus even said, that a man's righteousness must be as the Father's righteousness, as evidenced by love for Him and others.[37] It is the fact that we cannot do what is righteous that must drive us to Jesus Christ. It is the fact that we are so impoverished of spirit that should convict us of judgment. That is the point of the Gospel.

However paradoxical that may seem, however counterintuitive that may seem, and however that may affront

---

[35] John 3:19; this verse, as will be explained later, introduces a comparison between one thing and another. This is the comparison of love for darkness and love for Light. It is not so much that men loved darkness rather than the light, but that men love darkness *more than* light. That superlative comparison here by our Lord is incredible.

[36] See Genesis 1:26; cf. Romans 3:23.

[37] Matthew 5:21-48; esp. v.48.

our sense of what is right, it is the beginning of the gospel of Jesus Christ nonetheless. The Lord taught that Israel must repent of their sins, both individually (Matthew 4:17), and nationally (Matthew 10:5-6). They must repent; otherwise, God will not bring upon them the blessings of the covenant of promise to Abraham (Leviticus 26:40-41). Not only did Israel not repent, but they couldn't! In fact, like every other person, they are in a condition that is normally entitled "Depravity." This is the condition of heart, mind, and body that is less than God's glory, the very glory for which God made man (Romans 3:23). The Bible describes this condition as willful, purposeful, and permanent.[38] In fact, to be blunt, it is impossible to change man's condition. Indeed, it would take a miracle.

Returning to the serpent on the pole, which is the paradoxical dilemma facing the nation of Israel, they are to look at a replica of the very thing that bit them and got them into fatal trouble. However, the issue is not the serpent, nor the pole, nor even Moses. The issue is God's instructions. This replication is unlike the fascination with snakes that other cultures have, even the Ancient Near Eastern (ANE) cultures of Moses' day. Most cultures who revered snakes would wear a replica of them on a necklace, bracelet, or some other charm in order to "ward-off" snakes or evil spirits while walking the desert. Dennis Cole writes concerning this very fact,

---

[38] Ephesians 2:1-3, 11-12

75

"...there existed a paradox of function here as was true in the case of most of animal sacrifices for sin and guilt in the Israelite system. Blood, which by contact could render one unclean, could on the other hand bring ritual purification. This paradox is no more vividly pictured than in the ritual of the red cow (Numbers 19:1–22), whereby purification is affected for a person made unclean by death through the sprinkling of that which has rendered everyone else impure. So looking with hope for salvation and healing upon a form of that which has rendered one in a position of living or dying was a wondrously paradoxical act of faith in a God who controlled all power over life or death."[39]

The point he is making is the same as we see in this event in Numbers 21 and becomes the very crux of the matter with Nicodemus. He will also be faced with a paradoxical, contradictory, condition for eternal life—to be born from above. As impossible as this seems, it is the only way into the kingdom of heaven. This birth from above actually negates the physical birth of which Nicodemus is so proud.

The Israelites looking at the serpent on the pole would be doing something both impossible and yet necessary in order to live after being bitten. Only those who believe God would do it. How do I know that? Because the command was so impossible, even foolish-sounding, that man would see it as laughable. Much like the cross of Jesus Christ, looking at a serpent on a pole is foolishness to those Israelites who would not believe, but life to those who would (1 Corinthians 1:18-25).

In the text of Numbers 21 is a tremendous key that gives us the solution to this dilemma of man doing something of which he is incapable. The key is found in v. 9. In this verse, there is a

[39] R. Dennis Cole, vol. 3B, Numbers, The New American Commentary (Nashville: Broadman & Holman Publishers, 2000), 350.

Hebrew verb that does not carry the normal sense of a basic verb. It would have been easy for Moses simply to write the verb in the way it appears in English. That is, it would be easy for Moses to write, "when he looked to the bronze serpent, he lived." It reads in the English that a man will look at the serpent and then live. However, in Hebrew, the verb translated above as "look" is not a simple action that a person does. It is an action that is written in such a way that the person is *caused* to look. In Hebrew, you can have a verb carry a sense[40] depending upon what the writer is attempting to communicate. A perfect verb (Qal stem) would indicate a normal action that is usually a simple statement.[41] However, if you wanted to communicate that a person did something because something outside of him caused him to do it, you would use the Hiphil stem[42] of the Hebrew verb. Therefore, understanding that, you would read this verse this way: "...*when he was caused to look* to the bronze serpent, he lived." Do you see the difference? The people who were bitten must be *caused* to look to the serpent. Those who did, lived. How did you know if they were caused to look? Because they looked and they were alive afterwards. This significance is massive, especially as it relates to Jesus speaking

---

[40] See Nehemiah 8:8 for an example of this consideration.

[41] Robert B. Chisholm, Jr. *From Exegesis to Exposition* (Grand Rapids: Baker, 1998), p. 79.

[42] Bill T. Arnold, John H. Choi, *A Guide to Biblical Hebrew Syntax* (Cambridge: Cambridge University Press, 2003), pp. 48-49. See footnote 31 for more listings.

with Nicodemus, and as it relates to our understanding of receiving eternal life.

With that in mind, you can see that there really should have been 100% fatality. Nevertheless, there wasn't. Some people lived after being bitten. However, they did not live because they responded with obedience from within themselves and looked. Instead, they were *caused to look* as a result of God's work in their hearts to want to obey. Otherwise, none would have made it. A person lived because they were caused to obey God's instructions, as paradoxical as that may seem.

Now, with all that understood, let's go back to Nicodemus. Jesus told Nicodemus that just as the serpent was raised up by Moses, so must the Son of Man be raised also. We know that Jesus did not understand Moses' raising the serpent on the pole any different from the way that Moses wrote it. Jesus understood the text in Numbers 21 and the meaning was the same for Him as for Moses, and the same for us. Therefore, the correlation that Nicodemus must make at this point is that Jesus and the serpent have similarities. Moreover, those similarities are defined by Moses' raising of the serpent on the pole (bearing in mind that Christ Himself had not yet been "lifted up"[43]). What God did there by means of the sending of the snakes, the instructions to Moses for the snake replica, and the deliverance

---

[43] This phrase "lifted up" is a euphemism for death. Jesus would go on to teach that He must be "lifted up" because that is how He will demonstrate Himself as the Messiah (John 8:28) and draw all men unto Himself, by means of lordship (John 12:32). Therefore, here He is already predicting His death and resurrection.

of some who believed and obeyed because of God's gracious choice, patterns in some way Jesus Christ and His work as well.

We will learn in the next section exactly what that work is.

THE CROSS[44]

Central to the faith of the true Christian is the cross of Jesus Christ. This sounds, to some, like a morbid thought. However, it truly is at the core of Christianity. The preaching of the cross is our content and motivation for every activity we have as Christians. Many Christians are familiar with Paul's summary message to the Corinthians, "For I determined to know nothing among you except Jesus Christ and Him crucified" (1 Corinthians 2:2). Paul, as an apostle of the Lord Jesus Christ, had this commission and he spent his life fulfilling this calling. This is also the message of every Christian. This message brings conviction, enlightenment, repentance, and faith. It is the message of the church and it is different from any other message in existence. This is why Jesus spoke to Nicodemus the way that He did. Jesus' teaching was not like the rabbis'. Rather, His message was filled with authority and wisdom. It was His preaching and teaching that moved entire villages to desire His death (Luke 4:16-30), and entire villages to be redeemed (John 4:39-42). To some, He was the scourge of the land. To others, Jesus was life incarnate. This dichotomy of views is the same today. To some, the cross of Christ is ridiculous and abhorrent. They despise its message and hate the One who died upon it. However, to others, their hearts are melted by it and thus are granted life. Therefore, as we will see, the death of Christ on that

---

[44] It is helpful to refer to Don Green's thorough article in The Master's Seminary Journal entitled, "The Folly of the Cross," volume 15:1 (2004) for a description of the history, significance, and reality of the shame of what the Lord Jesus Christ endured on the cross.

cross is the life of those who are already dead. These realities are the "paradoxes" of the cross.

As Christians, we realize that our announcement to the world is the cross of Jesus Christ. The wooden "T-shaped" altar upon which the Lamb of God was crucified is the point of the message. However, this is more than a simple icon of the efforts of a religious teacher. It is more than the place where we idolize the One who died there in some fashion. In fact, it is more than simply telling people about the horrific events that occurred upon that cross. Remember, the lifting up of Jesus Christ on that cross corresponds to the lifting up of the serpent on the pole. The cross and its message, the very message that caused the death of Christ and all His apostles, are correlated to that serpent upon the pole. That is Jesus' point. He said to Nicodemus, "*As* Moses lifted up the serpent in the wilderness, *even so* must the Son of Man be lifted up..." Notice that the sentence begins with the word "As." In the Greek, that word is like saying, "in the same way." It is an adverb which describes comparison between two objects. In this case, Jesus is compared with the serpent. Or, more exactly, *the lifting up of* Jesus is compared with *the lifting up* of the serpent. Notice again that the Lord said that in the same way that the serpent was lifted up by Moses, so also, in that same way, must the Son of Man be lifted up. Thus, they are to be compared together.

Another instance of that word might serve to illustrate for us the idea here. In Luke 11:29-30, Jesus is reproving the

Jews for their incessant desire for signs. He says that they will not receive the signs *they* want, but He will give a sign that *He* wants to give. It is a sign related to the sign of a previous generation. A sign is a statement or pattern of something that is presented before people for a specific reason. In this case, the sign of the prophet Jonah serves to relate to the sign of Jesus Christ. Jonah was a preacher from whose ministry an entire town repented (Luke 11:32). His preaching was a sign to the town of the announcement that they should repent and fear God or else they would be overthrown (Jonah 3:1-10). That preaching was a sign to Nineveh and they repented. Likewise, Jesus Christ came as a sign to Israel. However, they did not repent at His preaching. Nevertheless, the actual persons of Jonah and Christ are signs by virtue of their preaching. In the same way, the serpent being lifted up corresponds to the lifting up of the Son of God so that all who look to Him might have life. The pole upon which Christ was lifted was the cross. Only those "caused" to look to Him will live. The rest will perish.

Nicodemus does not understand any of this. Not that it is difficult or complex. It is actually very simple. However, the profound nature of what it means is impossible to be grasp by the darkened mind. Further, Nicodemus would not completely understand all that the cross means either, but true Christians can because we are on this side of the cross. Therefore, a short survey of the cross in the New Testament is in order so that we might better appreciate its purpose.

God's Cross

"Men of Israel, listen to these words: Jesus the Nazarene, a man attested to you by God with miracles and wonders and signs which God performed through Him in your midst, just as you yourselves know—this Man, delivered over by the predetermined plan and foreknowledge of God, you nailed to a cross by the hands of godless men and put Him to death. But God raised Him up again, putting an end to the agony of death, since it was impossible for Him to be held in its power." (Acts 2:22-24)

In God's plan, the cross of Jesus Christ was central. It was the predetermined plan of God established by His sovereign foreknowledge. God planned it from before time, before Genesis 1:1, and His plan was right on schedule as His Son was hung on the cross by the hands of godless men. It was upon this cross that the Son of God would pay the penalty of the sins of all who would believe in Him. There He absorbed the wrath of God and satisfied God's punishment of death promised to Adam in the garden. It was there that the shame of death and humiliation was accompanied by the disgrace of the Father turning away from Him. All of this was the predetermined plan of God according to His perfect and fixed foreknowledge.

Historically, the use of a cross as a form of punishment for crimes was carried down from previous nations to the Romans[45] who used crucifixion extensively to maintain order. If

---

[45] "It seems that the Persians invented or first used this mode of execution. They probably did so in order not to defile the earth, which was consecrated to Ormuzd, by the body of the person executed. Later the cross is used by Alexander the Great, the Diadochoi princes and esp.

disorder ensued for any reason, the threat of crucifixion was imposed and thus only the offenders of "peace" would end up on the cross to die.[46] The actual act of crucifying a person is horrific to consider. With arms outstretched, the offender was either strapped to a wooden crossbeam or nailed to it, usually in the wrist and foot instep. The use of the cross for punishment was in force until Constantine removed it from use in honor of Jesus Christ. It was written of him that

"he regarded the cross with peculiar reverence, on account both of the power which it conveyed to him in the battles against his enemies, and also of the divine manner in which the symbol had appeared to him. He took away by law the crucifixion customary among the Romans, from the usage of the courts. He commanded that this divine symbol should always be inscribed and stamped

---

the Carthaginians, Polyb., 1, 24. From these it came to the Romans, who called the instrument used the *crux*. In Greece this punishment was restricted to slaves, cf. the Amyzon inscr. from Caria, BMI, IV, 2. No. 1036 (2nd/1st cent. b.c.); it was never even considered for free Greeks, Diod. S., 16, 54, 4. Only barbarians crucified free men, Hdt., I, 128; IV, 43 etc. In Rome it was already a mode of executing slaves even in the days of the republic. In the imperial period it was regarded as *servile supplicium* but was also used on aliens who were not Roman citizens. It could not be imposed on citizens, Cic. Verr., II, 5, 62, 162–165. But autocratic governors ignored this." *Theological Dictionary of the New Testament*, vol. 7 ed. Gerhard Kittel, Geoffrey W. Bromiley and Gerhard Friedrich, electronic ed. (Grand Rapids, MI: Eerdmans, 1964-), 573.

[46] "In the Roman provinces the penalty of crucifixion was one of the strongest means of maintaining order and security. Governors imposed this servile punishment esp. on freedom fighters who tried to break away from Roman rule." TDNT, vol.7, p.573.

whenever coins and images should be struck, and his images,
which exist in this very form, still testify to this order."[47]

The use of the cross, or the act of crucifixion was so horrendous that it was revered in its own category of torture. Thus, every culture abhorred this activity, and rightfully so.

What is important to comprehend, however, in discussing the cross is the shame accompanied with it. The stigma of being elevated above others in such a public way, which sometimes would be accompanied by nakedness, was very disgraceful and, in that culture, would usually not be spoken of in normal conversation. You can see this in the comments that some were hurling at Christ as He hung there:

> *"At that time two robbers were crucified with Him, one on the right and one on the left. And those passing by were hurling abuse at Him, wagging their heads and saying, "You who are going to destroy the temple and rebuild it in three days, save Yourself! If You are the Son of God, come down from the cross."*
>
> *In the same way the chief priests also, along with the scribes and elders, were mocking Him and saying, "He saved others; He cannot save Himself. He is the King of Israel; let Him now come down from the cross, and we will believe in Him." "He trusts in God; let God rescue Him now, if He delights in Him; for He said, 'I am the Son of God.' " The robbers who had been crucified with Him were also insulting Him with the same words" (Matthew 27:38-44).*

---

[47] Sozomen, "The Ecclesiastical History of Salaminius Hermias Sozomenus", trans. Chester D. Hartranft In, in *A Select Library of the Nicene and Post-Nicene Fathers of the Christian Church, Second Series, Volume II: Socrates, Sozomenus: Church Histories*, ed. Philip Schaff and Henry Wace (New York: Christian Literature Company, 1890), 245.

The Serpent and the Cross

One inscription exists of a man hanging on a cross with another man below him worshiping him. That, in itself, as strange as it might be, would not seem so bad. However, the man on the cross is drawn having a donkey's head and below the drawing is written, "Alexamenos worships his god."[48] The sneering and contempt at the foolishness of worshiping someone upon a cross in that day was normal. Christians in the early days of the church were the ridicule of the pagans for such stupidity as to worship a man who obviously was accursed by the gods.

Paul relayed the fact of disgrace for those who were upon the cross in Galatians 3:13. There Paul quotes Deuteronomy 21:23 and iterates that even God deems one who is hung on a tree or stake as being a defiling disgrace and should not remain there overnight so as not to begin the new day under its shadow. The cross was disgraceful for man and God and was by no means a usual consideration of anyone. It was filled with the stigma of the disgrace of man's contempt and the due course of the crime one has committed.

That is the problem—Jesus Christ committed no crime. His death upon one of man's most horrific torture tools was an even greater atrocity than the act of crucifixion itself. He did not deserve to die. It was there that man rejected Him and it was there that the Father turned His face away from His Son to bear

---

[48] Roland Bainton, *The Church of Our Fathers* (Salem, Ohio: Schmul Publishing, 1987), 22.

the shame of the cross utterly alone.[49] Isaiah prophesied of this rejection of man and God in the fifty-third chapter of his prophecy:

> He was despised and forsaken of men,
> A man of sorrows and acquainted with grief;
> And like one from whom men hide their face
> He was despised, and we did not esteem Him.
> Surely our griefs He Himself bore,
> And our sorrows He carried;
> Yet we ourselves esteemed Him stricken,
> Smitten of God, and afflicted...
> But the Lord was pleased
> To crush Him, putting Him to grief;
> If He would render Himself as a guilt offering,
> He will see His offspring,
> He will prolong His days,
> And the good pleasure of the Lord will prosper in His hand.
> (Isaiah 53:3-10)

Our Cross

"And He was saying to them all, "If anyone wishes to come after Me, he must deny himself, and take up his cross daily and follow Me." (Luke 9:23)

The verse above makes better sense once understood from the standpoint of the offensive nature of the cross and crucifixion in general. In order to go where Jesus is going, we

---

[49] See Psalm 22:1; cp. Matthew 27:46; Mark 15:34.

must be willing to bear our own level of shame and contempt from the world such that they would laugh, mock, and sneer at us for following Christ. However, the result is glory for us and condemnation for them. Nevertheless, we must be willing to face the contempt of the world at this time in order to follow Jesus Christ.

This is a tall order for us for a number of reasons: pride, love of the world, love of people.

Our pride despises the idea of self-crucifixion. The idea of denying the flesh and putting it in a position of death in this world is repulsive to our own love of self. We want to exalt and promote ourselves, not die. Furthermore, we really like this world. All of its allurements, pleasures, and joys, are simply there for the asking. Whether it is the internet, television programs, literature, or our own pursuit of what is sinful, we love it and want it in any medium we can get it. For a person to deny himself that kind of pleasure is inconceivable for us. However, not only do we love ourselves, we "love" people too. I am not speaking of godly love of others. Rather, I mean the "love" of persons who "love" us back. In other words, we love the accolades of men. We want to please the person next to us in order to get a pat on the back, and we crave recognition and congratulation. The Academy Awards is the epitome of self-congratulation and prideful, cultural recognition. To demand that a person endure the rejection of these same people is simply too much for us. If we don't receive the accolades from The Academy, or any other group for that matter, who will recognize our accomplishments and us? This proud people-pleasing makes it impossible for us to understand the recognition which we find in Christ.

In Christ, we gain recognition from the Father (Matthew 6:1-8). However, this is not recognition for being such a wonderful, amazing, good individual. Rather, it is recognition of the righteousness of His Son, which has been placed upon His children and continually sanctifies them. Truly, that is a far better recognition than Him looking at our depraved selves. However, this recognition comes at the price of public mockery and disgrace. So, the question is: are you willing to pay that price?

Paul wrote in Galatians 2:20

"I have been crucified with Christ; and it is no longer I who live, but Christ lives in me; and the life which I now live in the flesh I live by faith in the Son of God, who loved me and gave Himself up for me.

He understood what it meant to bear his cross. Paul understood that he was crucified to the world and the world to him, such that he was willing to endure the cross so that he might live by faith in the Son of God. Paul made himself despicable to the world, not by being obtuse to the world through a self-made religion, but rather by simply believing and obeying what Jesus taught. This kind of assault (although we don't normally view it as such) was unwelcome to the world and despised. Paul knew that, but it simply did not matter to him.

The Serpent and the Cross

Jesus Christ loved him and He gave Himself up for him. So, who was Paul to deny Christ? With gratitude to God, Paul lived happily with the scorn of the world. He wrote in 1 Corinthians 4:9–13,

"For, I think, God has exhibited us apostles last of all, as men condemned to death; because we have become a spectacle to the world, both to angels and to men. We are fools for Christ's sake, but you are prudent in Christ; we are weak, but you are strong; you are distinguished, but we are without honor. To this present hour we are both hungry and thirsty, and are poorly clothed, and are roughly treated, and are homeless; and we toil, working with our own hands; when we are reviled, we bless; when we are persecuted, we endure; when we are slandered, we try to conciliate; we have become as the scum of the world, the dregs of all things, even until now."

His position as apostle meant nothing to this world. In fact, who cares if a man is a follower of a crucified Man? "The fool who would do that should be condemned to death and become a spectacle to the world. These men really are the scum, off-scouring, of the world," they say. Because of Paul and his "foolishness," he was beheaded a few years after writing this. To some, this was a waste of a perfectly good life. I do not mean Paul's death was a waste of a perfectly good life, but the way he lived. I could imagine the disgrace he endured being an heir to Gamaliel, the highest Rabbi of the land, a Pharisee of Pharisees, and the perfect specimen of the Hebrews.[50] To men, his was a wasted life. To God, it was the most commendable one.

This is the cross. The cross of Jesus Christ calls us to suffer as He did. Surely, we cannot suffer for our sins and atone for them, for that was accomplished by Christ once and for all time. However, as Peter says, "Therefore, since Christ has suffered in the flesh, arm yourselves also with the same purpose, because he who has suffered in the flesh has ceased from sin" (1 Peter 4:1). Those who suffer as Christ did, which is a reference to His crucifixion and the shame accompanied with it, will also beat back the impulses of the flesh. This is no indication that a believer is to be crucified, although many Christians under Roman Emperor Nero were.[51] The suffering of Christ was also about the scorn of the shame of the cross. The derision that He endured is ours as well (Hebrews 13:12–13). Our suffering for righteousness must include the ridicule of the very men we are trying to reconcile to God. Nevertheless, we endure it, take it, and are patient with it so that we might also be triumphant over it in the future.

Nicodemus would have no idea about any of this as the Lord was speaking to him. The concept of receiving contempt from the fellow Pharisees was unthinkable. The Pharisees were known for their parade of righteousness in the marketplace and in the streets of the cities. Pharisees did all that they did in order to be noticed of men. Jesus exposed them correctly:

---

[50] Philippians 3:4-6; cf. Acts 22:3
[51] Bainton, p.22

"Then Jesus spoke to the crowds and to His disciples, saying: "The scribes and the Pharisees have seated themselves in the chair of Moses; therefore all that they tell you, do and observe, but do not do according to their deeds; for they say things and do not do them. They tie up heavy burdens and lay them on men's shoulders, but they themselves are unwilling to move them with so much as a finger. But they do all their deeds to be noticed by men; for they broaden their phylacteries and lengthen the tassels of their garments. They love the place of honor at banquets and the chief seats in the synagogues, and respectful greetings in the market places, and being called Rabbi by men" (Matthew 23:1-7).

All of their righteousness was compared with other Pharisees and men in the marketplace. The places of honor, chief seats, and respectful greetings by men were coveted: the more the better. For a Pharisee to receive Jesus Christ as Son of God and Messiah was to turn your back on the accolades of the men with whom you have spent your life comparing yourself. It is to reject the structure of righteousness that you have worked hard to erect and it is to receive the scorn of those men who once gave you praise. Apparently, like most people, Nicodemus was not willing to endure—not yet.[52]

---

[52] John 7:13; 9:22; 12:42-43; 19:38-39; 20:19

Chapter 6

THE SON OF MAN

Although we have introduced this reference to the "Son of Man," it is imperative that we develop it more here. Twice in this passage, verses 13 and 14, the phrase "the Son of Man" is used by the Lord.[53] Because the Lord repeats the phrase indicates that it has some significance to the understanding of Jesus' teaching here. We will now take some time in this chapter to examine this phrase and see what further significance there must be. We will find that understanding Jesus Christ as the Son of Man is vastly significant to Nicodemus' understanding of the Man with whom he is speaking on that warm Spring night.

As we attempt to collect the teaching about the Son of Man from Scripture, we find ourselves swimming in the deep end. The concept is vast and profound. Jesus, using this title, is opening a door that, I believe, completely rocked the foundations of Nicodemus' belief to the core. Here He is—the Son of Man, speaking with this religious leader. Nicodemus is face to face with the Son and he did not know it. He would eventually know it, come to the Son, and receive life. But for now, he was in the dark until Christ shined the light of knowledge upon Nicodemus' dark mind.

---

[53] "Son of Man" is referred to 13x's in the Gospel of John.

The title "Son of Man" comes most directly from Daniel 7:9-14. In that passage, Daniel is given a powerful vision. The picture is of the future when the Ancient of Days (God the Father) sits upon His throne to judge, as well as multiple thrones around Him witnessing His judgment. He is brilliant and glorious, and after His regal entrance, the court sat and the books were opened (v. 10b). Jumping to v. 13, we see that one comes to Him and was presented before Him. It was to this One that glory, dominion and an indestructible kingdom (Hebrews 12:25-29) was given. The peoples of the earth would serve Him, and would do so forever!

Yet, the question comes to mind, "Why was He given this kingdom?" Sure, God can give a kingdom to anyone He pleases. And sure, God loves His Son and would give to Him what He wills. Yet, there must be some kind of reason for this incredible gift. Something must have motivated God beyond simple niceties. I believe there was something motivating God, and for that we must turn further back into the Old Testament to Psalm chapter 2.

PSALM 2-THE PSALM OF THE KINGDOM

We have already been introduced to Psalm 2 in chapter 2 of this book. That overview serves to begin our consideration of the dialogue between the Father and the Son. However, now, we must return to it and amplify the truths there, especially as they relate to Jesus Christ as the Son of Man.

The concept of the "Son of Man" is that One is made like a man. That is, he is birthed and raised in the way a man is birthed and raised—in a human body. Every male who has ever lived is the son of some man. However, to be *the* Son of Man is different from that. The significance is that this Son of Man is also the Son of God. That is, the Son of God became the Son of Man. This fact, and how it came to be and why, is the point of the Lord's teaching.

Remember that God had instructed the Son to ask of Him for nations and the earth. This is the "decree" of the LORD (vv. 7-9). The decree is the entire conversation of the Son and Father and it is the overarching decree that moves all history. What I mean is this decree ('You are My Son, today I have begotten You. Ask of Me, and I will surely give the nations as Your inheritance, and the very ends of the earth as Your possession. You shall break them with a rod of iron, You shall shatter them like earthenware,') is the reason for creation, the fall, redemption, and re-creation. Although some theologians see pre-creation covenants between the Father and the Son, this Psalm verifies that there are no covenants at all.[54] The Son is instructed by the Father to ask for something, and the Father carries out the request of the Son in real time and history. To see this as a covenant is to reduce God to a level of stricture and regulation within the godhead. All that we understand about the godhead

---

[54] See appendix 2

indicates otherwise. Jesus said, "Father, I desire that they also, whom You have given Me, be with Me where I am, so that they may see My glory which You have given Me, for You loved Me before the foundation of the world" (John 17:24). By Christ's own admission, love was expressed to the Son by the Father at the time when He decreed to give people to the Son. It was love that motivated the Father to give gifts of men, redeemed men, to the Son. It was love for the Son that caused the Father to predestine some to believe in the Son and receive eternal life. It was love, not a covenant.

The kingdom is for the Son, and those who are redeemed by the Father are the kingdom. Remember, God instructed the Son to ask for the nations and the earth when as yet there were neither. No nation existed and the earth was not yet made. That conversation occurred in eternity past and explains why anything exists at all. To understand these realities is to understand the kingdom of God, and to understand the kingdom of God in this manner is to understand why, apart from perfect righteousness, no man can enter it. This kingdom, which the Father promised to the Son as a result of the request of the Son, is eternal and represents the very perfections of God Himself.

We must work back from the future in order to grasp the grandeur of these things. Let's take some time now and examine further the kingdom of the Son of Man.

THE KINGDOM OF THE SON OF MAN

Jesus taught of His kingdom from the beginning of His ministry to the end. At the beginning of His ministry He announced that the kingdom of heaven was at hand (Matthew 4:17). He was announcing that the Son is now present to receive His kingdom and to purge the stumbling blocks from it (Matthew 13:41). The announcement to the world that His kingdom is impending is to announce that all men must repent from their sins and turn to the King. David declared as much in Psalm 2 when he wrote,

> *"Now therefore, O kings, show discernment; take warning, O judges of the earth. Worship the Lord with reverence and rejoice with trembling. Do homage to the Son, that He not become angry, and you perish in the way, for His wrath may soon be kindled. How blessed are all who take refuge in Him!" (vv. 7-12).*

All the kings and subjects of the earth, especially His people Israel, must bow before the King. Otherwise, He will come in His fury and destroy the kings and nations that do not pay homage[55] to the Son.

---

[55] Literally, "kiss the Son" נַשְּׁקוּ־בַ֫ר . the word for "Son" here is not the normal Hebrew word for son, בֵּן,used in v. 7. Rather, it is the Aramaic word בַּר, "son." It is fascinating that David wrote it this way. What it probably indicates is a call to the gentilic (non-Israelite)

Throughout His ministry, the kingdom was the focus. His preaching was of the gospel of the kingdom (Matthew 4:23). His teaching was about the components of the qualities of entrance and existence in that kingdom.[56] He taught that the kingdom is with power, as demonstrated by the casting out of demons, healings, and miracles (Matthew 12:28). The keys to entrance into the kingdom were given to the apostles, and by progress of time and extension of that authority, to the church in general. That is, we know what it takes to enter the kingdom as it has been revealed to us through Christ and His apostles (Matthew 16:19). Seeking after that kingdom is the preoccupation of His children (Luke 12:31). At this time, the kingdom has been taken from Israel and presented to the nations as a result of the refusal of Israel to repent of her sins (Matthew 21:43). In the progress of the inauguration of the kingdom of the Son, Israel will repent and fulfill all her covenant obligations. However, for now, they are partially blinded and hardened (Romans 11:25-27).

There is one particular parable about the kingdom that requires special attention, however, because it explains so much. Remember, since Nicodemus was the teacher of Israel, he really should have understood what we just reviewed. But he did not. As we examine the kingdom further, we will find that there is

---

nations, as represented by the utilization of an Aramaic (non-Hebraic) term, to obey the command-"kiss the Son."
[56] Matthew 5:3-20. In fact, all the Sermon on the Mount summarizes life in the Kingdom of the Son.

more that he must comprehend if he is to know the Son of Man, the Heir of the kingdom.

THE KINGDOM PARABLES

Matthew 13 is a monumental chapter detailing not only the history of the kingdom in the world, but also its culmination. This chapter is situated in the middle of the Lord's ministry and it is actually the result of the hard-heartedness of the Jews toward Christ. They have been calling Him Lord of the Flies since chapter 9 verse 34, thus attributing His works to demons and Satan. They have ridiculed Him and wanted Him dead for quite some time. He has been preaching redemption and the kingdom of God to the masses and calling His people to Himself, in spite of the efforts of the wicked Pharisees.

The beginning of chapter 13 indicates that Jesus has turned away from the Pharisees and hidden from them the truths concerning the nature of the kingdom. Verse 11 indicates that the disciples have now become the students of the kingdom in order to understand its manifold riches, and the others (the Pharisees and their followers) are now blinded by their own ignorance. Jesus has removed His truth from them and the door to the kingdom is shut. In this chapter, Jesus explains the kingdom in terms that were completely unlike what they expected. They had not conceived of a kingdom that encompassed the world (vv. 31-32). They had not conceived of a kingdom that is of such a quality that it must be found and sought after (vv. 44-46). They had never considered a kingdom that had as its announcement method the scattering of seeds (vv. 3-9, 18-23). This was all new.

Yet, there is one parable in particular that stands out of the rest as to its explanation of the kingdom and that is the parable of the wheat and the tares.

THE PARABLE OF THE WHEAT AND THE TARES

The Kingdom of Heaven is the topic of the thirteenth chapter of Matthew. The Jews have rejected Jesus Christ, refused to repent, and thus the kingdom promised to them through Abraham culminating in David's covenant,[57] was unavailable to them. As a result, the kingdom of Jesus Christ, in a form not revealed in the Old Testament, was given to the nations. This kingdom, the rulership of the Lord Jesus Christ both in time and eternity, is thus made available to the nations of the world. This is in accord with the eternal plan of God, as Paul wrote, "This was in accordance with the eternal purpose which He carried out in Christ Jesus our Lord..." (Ephesians 3:11). This purpose was "hidden in God" (Ephesians 3:9) and is now revealed to the apostles and prophets of the Lord Jesus Christ because of God's temporary rejection of Israel. This kingdom is the subject of the

---

[57] 2 Samuel 7:13-16; cf. Psalm 89:35-37.

Christian gospel. In fact, its' message *is* the gospel of the Lord Jesus Christ.

If, as we saw in the previous conversation, the kingdom of God was prepared for the Son by the Father, then how did it come to be in the condition we find it in now? That is, where did sin, death, and decay come from? The Parable of the Wheat and the Tares answers that question. Let's look at it.

"Jesus presented another parable to them, saying, "The kingdom of heaven may be compared to a man who sowed good seed in his field. But while his men were sleeping, his enemy came and sowed tares among the wheat, and went away. But when the wheat sprouted and bore grain, then the tares became evident also. The slaves of the landowner came and said to him, 'Sir, did you not sow good seed in your field? How then does it have tares?' And he said to them, 'An enemy has done this!' The slaves *said to him, 'Do you want us, then, to go and gather them up?' But he *said, 'No; for while you are gathering up the tares, you may uproot the wheat with them. 'Allow both to grow together until the harvest;' and in the time of the harvest I will say to the reapers, 'First gather up the tares and bind them in bundles to burn them up; but gather the wheat into my barn' " (vv. 24-30).

In summary, the parable proceeds like this: a man sows some seeds of wheat into a field and goes away. Another man, an enemy of the first man, comes and sows seeds of false wheat (tares) into the man's field. As time goes along, it becomes evident that someone has sown weeds into the field to grow along with the wheat. However, they can't be separated until the harvest. At that time, the weeds will go to the burn pile and the wheat sent to the mill.

Jesus explains this parable for his newly enlightened disciples. He said,

"Then He left the crowds and went into the house. And His disciples came to Him and said, 'Explain to us the parable of the tares of the field.' And He said, 'The one who sows the good seed is the Son of Man, and the field is the world; and as for the good seed, these are the sons of the kingdom; and the tares are the sons of the evil one; and the enemy who sowed them is the devil, and the harvest is the end of the age; and the reapers are angels. So just as the tares are gathered up and burned with fire, so shall it be at the end of the age. The Son of Man will send forth His angels, and they will gather out of His kingdom all stumbling blocks, and those who commit lawlessness, and will throw them into the furnace of fire; in that place there will be weeping and gnashing of teeth. Then the righteous will shine forth as the sun in the kingdom of their Father. He who has ears, let him hear' " (vv. 36-43).

The components of the parable are given by the Lord in order to teach the disciples concerning the meaning of what He was trying to illustrate. He gives us the components as follows:

The sower is the Son of Man, the field is the world, the good seed are collectively the sons of the kingdom, the tares are the sons of the evil one, the enemy is the devil, the harvest is the end of the age and the reapers are angels. If we simply plug in the values for the equation, we have this: the Son of Man planted, at creation, the sons of the kingdom into the world. The enemy of God, Satan, came and planted into the world the children of the devil, by means of deceiving Eve, which are his followers. The dynamics presented here are fantastic and profound. However, the real impact of this parable is in the very first sentence of the parable, v. 24. It reads, "The kingdom of heaven may be compared to..." The verb in this part of the sentence is the verb "may be compared to." In Greek, it is better translated "was compared to."[58] This verb in this form has the sense of a past time event that started and stopped in time. Thus, we translate it, "The kingdom of heaven was (at some previous time) compared to a man who..." The other verbs in this chapter in reference to describing the kingdom of heaven are all present tense verbs.[59] But here the Lord is describing an event in the past that instructs us concerning the kingdom of heaven.

With that in mind, here is what we know. At creation, Jesus Christ, the Son of Man, began His kingdom by creating the world and everything in it.[60] This was in response to the Father initiating His plan by authorizing the Lord to do this. It is a result of the instructions from the Father to the Son to ask of Him for the nations and the earth. Therefore, the Son of God makes the universe, the earth, and the animals. He then creates man to populate the earth and to rule over it, with the woman as helper, in the manner prescribed in Genesis 1:26-28. This is the sowing of the sons of the kingdom in the parable, and is the kingdom prepared for the saints *from* the foundation of the world.[61] While Christ left the earth, Satan came down, having fallen from heaven, and tempted the woman, who in turn tempted the man

---

[58] The verb is "Ὡμοιώθη" which is an aorist passive verb.
[59] See vv. 31, 33, 44, 45, 47

[60] John 1:1-3; Colossians 1:16; Hebrews 1:1-2

[61] See Matthew 25:34

and the man disobeyed. Just after the fall, the Son of God comes to the earth and "discovers" what has happened. However, instead of judging the man and woman, He allows the wheat to coexist, as it were, alongside the tares of Satan's children.[62] We can see this reality in the first few chapters of Genesis as we see the "seed-line" of the sons of God, and the "seed-line" of the sons of the evil one side by side. Therefore, the world is heading for the judgment to come in which Jesus will separate the wheat and the tares; the sons of the kingdom and the sons of the evil one. Nevertheless, the kingdom, in the beginning, was (and continues to be) for the sons of God[63] and not for the sons of the evil one. However, there must come a day when Jesus will separate the good from the evil. Then His kingdom, planned by the Father for the Son from the beginning, will be His for eternity.[64]

This kingdom belongs to the Son of Man. It is His. It is given to Him by the Father and it is this kingdom that is in view in Daniel 7:9-14. The Son of Man will receive His kingdom from

---

[62] The concept of the sons of the evil one is a vast subject that is a foundational teaching in Scripture. Everyone from Cain to the last person to be born in history who rejects and disobeys God would be considered a son of the evil one. The reason this is so significant is because it allows for the distinction between the sons of the devil and the sons of the kingdom, the children of God. The sons of the devil can never be redeemed, as they are not sons of the kingdom as determined by the Father from eternity past. A foundational passage to discern this is located in 1 John 3:4-12

[63] See Luke 3:38 wherein Adam himself is called a "son of God."

[64] See Matthew 13:41-43; cf. Daniel 7:13-14

the Father and in that kingdom, He will gain the nations and the earth. This is why the disciples are told to go into all the world making disciples of all the nations (Matthew 28:18-20).[65] The nations belong to Jesus Christ, and He will come and receive them to Himself in God's time.

Nicodemus is speaking to this very Son of Man. He is the Heir of all things and He will claim them in the Father's time. Key to the plan of the Kingdom of God is the death of the Son for those who are His.

---

[65] See appendix 3

Chapter 7

Eternal Life

The Lord then told Nicodemus that, just as temporal death by the serpents is spared by looking to the serpent situated upon the pole, as a result of God "causing" one to look, so also a person is spared from eternal death by looking to the Son of Man who is lifted up on the pole of the cross. Remember, however, that the people were complaining unbelievers and really did not deserve to be saved from the serpent's bite. There really were not any in the group who were faithful to YHWH, except Moses, Joshua, and Caleb. The rest were getting exactly what they deserved-death.

Yet, God delivered some from temporal death. Some were "caused" to look to the enigmatic serpent fashioned upon the pole. True to the sign of the serpent and the replication of that sign by Jesus Christ and His death on the cross, only those caused to look to Jesus Christ will be saved. Eternal life, although not deserving, is the benefit of those who look to Christ.

From this point, Jesus teaches Nicodemus concerning life, death, and judgment. As we have seen, Nicodemus should have understood all of this already, but again we see that he is ignorant of them all. Now in the passage both eternal life and eternal death become the focal points. It would be good to bear in mind that eternal life is only for those who are compelled to look to Christ. Therefore, the rest of mankind will inevitably perish. The Lord will make this fact clear in the verses that follow.

THOSE WHO POSSESS LIFE

We now turn to what is usually considered the most well-known portion of the New Testament (if not the whole Bible). In this discussion, we will come to grasp verses 15-16 of John 3. The Lord's teaching culminates in an unequivocally dogmatic and profound statement about man's depraved inability and God's salvific ability. As such, this portion is deep, profound, and awe-inspiring.

In John 3:15-16, the Lord states that those who believe possess eternal life. Now, I am confident that the Lord's words mean exactly what they sound like: those who believe possess eternal life. However, it is crucial that we think carefully about what this means. Jesus said, "so that whoever believes will in Him have eternal life" (v.15). What is the Lord saying? What did He mean? Is this a blank check such that anyone who believes in Jesus will then, on the basis of their faith, receive eternal life? Or is there more to this statement, which is repeated in so many words in v. 16? I am confident that there is so much more in these verses than we often understand.[66]

I want to make a statement before we proceed further: I am not proposing a novel interpretation of this passage, but rather I am attempting to adhere the original one.[67] I believe that over the years, as can often happen, the actual meaning of this section of Scripture has been overshadowed by sincere and well-meaning persons who wish to see people saved.[68] Sadly, this emotion and good-will has undermined the proper understanding of the Lord's teaching, leaving most persons unaware of what this section truly means. Therefore, I will spend the remainder of this book interpreting these verses and explaining what doctrines they are teaching.

---

[66] See Appendix 4 concerning the exegetical information contained in these verses.

[67] A most helpful collection of studies on the history of the understanding of John 3:16, albeit from a strongly Reformed perspective, is in the web-resource, 'A Puritan's Mind' by Dr. C. Matthew McMahon. Although his perspective is heavily influenced by historic Reformed Theology (i.e. Covenant Theology), it does, nonetheless, represent considerable study on the historical interpretation of this verse. It can be found at http://www.apuritansmind.com/arminianism/an-exegetical-look-at-john-316-by-dr-c-matthew-mcmahon/ site accessed 1/15.2014.

[68] Interestingly, a perusal of Philip Schaff's *A Select Library of Nicene and Post-Nicene Fathers of the Christian Church*, (New York: Christian Literature Company, 1888) indicates that the predominant understanding of John 3:16 in the writings of the church fathers is that of what may be called "Arminian." That would be the understanding that the offer to true salvation is open to the world if they would only but receive it, disregarding the aspect of whom God has chosen or not chosen.

Let's begin with John 3:15. As mentioned, the Lord says that those who believe possess eternal life. A few important points need to be made now. First, notice the word "whoever." This word has the indication that eternal life belongs to those who believe. However, many take this to the nth degree and make it say that anyone and everyone who "believes" in Jesus can then gain eternal life This doctrine is most often espoused in evangelistic endeavors where the success of the endeavor is measured by the number of individual responses (moreover, what it means to *believe* is often left unexplained).[69] Yet, that is

---

[69] For example, Hank Hanegraff writes, "WHAT DOES IT MEAN TO BELIEVE IN JESUS CHRIST?- What is Belief?
This leads me to point number two — that a person also needs to exercise the proper type of belief. For example someone who holds to an accurate view of who Jesus Christ really is, and what the Bible says about Him, still needs to do something with his or her belief, and not simply stand by on the sidelines. True Christian belief is demonstrated through action. It isn't merely a passive acceptance of a set of doctrines (cf. James 2:19), but an active and dynamic relationship with Jesus Christ, trusting Him as personal Lord and Savior (Rom. 10:9; Titus 2:13). Christians are sinners saved by grace; and until a person has developed a saving relationship with the Jesus of the Bible, he or she, unlike true Christians, still remains dead in sin. In summary then, true biblical belief involves not only knowledge and agreement, but also trust. To demonstrate that one truly believes, we must trust in Jesus Christ alone for eternal life. (Hank Hanegraff, Christian Research Institute, http://www.equip.org/perspectives/what-does-it-mean-to-believe-in-jesus/ site accessed 12/30/2013). What is the problem with this kind of thinking? It is this: the source of the belief explained here is still the person. "A person also needs to exercise the proper type of belief...[faith] is an active and dynamic relationship with Jesus Christ, trusting Him as personal Lord and Savior...until a person has developed a saving relationship with the Jesus of the Bible, he or she, unlike true Christians, still remain dead in their sins." Nowhere in the New Testament are we told to trust in Jesus alone for salvation. He is the only provision for salvation. But, it is not about "trust." Jesus never called people to trust Him for salvation. He called them to repentance (Matthew 4:17), follow Him (Luke 9:59), belief (Mark 1:15), and fear (Luke 12:5). The verification that they truly believed was the ensuing

not what this verse is indicating, and the same holds true for v.16. What is found, however, is the following: "He who is a believing one." That is far different from "Whoever." In Greek, the language of the New Testament, there is a word for "whoever" and it is a compound relative pronoun. However, that is not the word used here. What is used here is the article, "the," along with a present participle.[70] What is the significance of this? The significance is that a participle describes a person. It is a present-time description of a man, a particular kind of man. What is significant about this person? He is one who is *currently* a believer, as indicated by the present tense of the participle. This person is not one who does not believe at first, but then believes and consequently is rewarded eternal life. Rather, this is a person who already believes and thus demonstrates the possession of eternal life. In other words, the person of v.15 is a person who already believes in Jesus Christ. Coupled with the present active subjunctive of "I have" toward the end of the verse, it indicates the purpose of God. That is, God's purpose is that the Son of Man be "lifted up" in order that those believing in Him would possess eternal life. Therefore, this is not a promise to someone that if they just believe in Jesus, they will then

---

obedience to Jesus' words (John 8:31-32). By no means are we the source of that belief. It is given of God and accompanies eternal life.

[70] The verse in Greek is: ἵνα πᾶς **ὁ πιστεύων** ἐν αὐτῷ ἔχῃ ζωὴν αἰώνιον (emphasis mine). The article with the participle is in bold. The indication here is that the person with eternal life is described as one who believes and keeps believing. This is true of every person who believes. This verse does not contain the relative pronoun, ὃς ἄν, which means "whoever," and neither does John 3:16.

receive eternal life. It is rather a description of the person who actually possesses eternal life, i.e. the believing one. Obviously, from other passages, we understand that men are commanded to believe in the gospel for salvation (Mark 1:15). However, John 3:15-16 is a description of one who possesses eternal life rather than how to get it.

JOHN 3:16

As we work through this verse, a number of factors to consider must be in place before we continue. First, remember that this is a conversation with a man named Nicodemus. This is not commentary from the Apostle John about this conversation. What is said in vv. 16-21 fits the conversation of the previous verses, which are clearly a dialogue between Christ and Nicodemus.[71] The conversation fits the flow of the previous verses, namely the lifting of the serpent on the pole. Also, it would be a bit stilted to insert what is said in vv. 16-21 between the discussion of vv. 10-15 and vv. 22 and following. In other words, it would not allow for the flow of thought as indicated by the phrase of v. 22, "After these things..." which is a typical Johannine phrase uniting what was happening before.[72] Finally,

---

[71] See Gerald L. Borchert, vol. 25A, *John 1–11*, The New American Commentary (Nashville: Broadman & Holman Publishers, 1996), Excursus 3, p.179.

[72] See John 5:1; 6:1; and 21:1, which presents the test case that if there is a switch in person in the verse, it will become evident within the verses themselves. That is, John writes the words of Christ in v. 29,

v. 16 begins with a conjunction that links it with v. 15 which itself is also integral to the previous two verses as well. Therefore, we take this section as all one conversation with Nicodemus, just as it stands in a Red-Lettered Bible.

Secondly, we must understand that this portion of the discussion flows from Jesus' teaching concerning Moses and the serpent in the wilderness from Numbers 21. We know this is the case because of the explanatory conjunction "For" at the beginning of v. 16. That conjunction carries through vv. 14-15. Therefore, John 3:16 *explains* the reality of the previous assertions made through vv. 14-15: if you see a man who believes, you are looking at a person who possesses eternal life, and is himself the beneficiary of the life and death of the Son of God. Jesus offers this explanation to Nicodemus so that he would comprehend entrance into the kingdom (see vv. 3 & 12). Again, only the person who believes shows that he already possesses eternal life.

Thirdly, realize that Nicodemus did not believe, since Jesus said as much in v. 12. Therefore, the profound considerations of vv. 16-21 presented to him are heavenly

---

since the verse is obviously from the perspective of Jesus Himself. The next verse is not written from the perspective of the Lord, but of the author of the book, John, since he speaks of Jesus by name and relates to his audience as "you." You will also note that v. 1 of chapter 21 gives cohesion to the previous section by using the phrase, "After these things." However, this still allows for different speakers within two verses, yet the difference in speakers is obvious from the verses themselves.

realities, and did not produce belief at that time. However, these seeds were planted and ultimately took root later on (see John 19:38-42).

(see John 19:38-42).

BREAKING IT DOWN

As we work through John 3:16 so we can appreciate the Lord's words there, we must take the time to break it down into parts and rebuild it. This is not done so that we can re-define it erroneously; it is to examine the whole in light of the parts. In doing so, we cannot assume that Scripture is not up to this task. Therefore, I am confident that once we have the parts understood as written, the whole will be understood as well.

"For God so loved the world..."

For most people, this phrase will immediately evoke a rush of emotion. Gerald Borchert, in his commentary of the Gospel of John, writes of the usual consideration of this love:

John saw Jesus as the answer to the world's need. The people of the world were the focus of God's love in Jesus (3:16). [73]

The sense that God would love us is a wonderful reality of Scripture. God's love[74] is an immense and variegated truth of

---

[73] Gerald L. Borchert, vol. 25A, *John 1–11*, The New American Commentary (Nashville: Broadman & Holman Publishers, 1996), 216.

the written Word. We see the idea of it in verses like, *"But God demonstrates His own love toward us, in that while we were yet sinners, Christ died for us"* (Romans 5:8). And, *"Nevertheless, the Lord your God was not willing to listen to Balaam, but the Lord your God turned the curse into a blessing for you because the Lord your God loves you"* (Deuteronomy 23:5). And again, *"Just as it is written, "Jacob I loved, but Esau I hated"* (Romans 9:13). Or, *"In this is love, not that we loved God, but that He loved us and sent His Son to be the propitiation for our sins"* (1 John 4:10). The reality of the love of God is the very reality of the godhead: the Father loves the Son (John 17:24), the Son loves the Father (John 14:31). The Spirit loves both and is loved by both (1 John 4:7-8).

This love is a love that makes up God Himself. It is selfless, pure, and holy, expressing itself in giving (Acts 20:35) and holy kindness. It is a love that willingly sacrifices itself to the benefit of others. In us, it is a love that understands the supremacy of God and bows before it.

As we read John 3:16, we can appreciate the love of God as it stands. However, we must examine further how the word "love" is used in this phrase "For God so *loved* the world." By examining this, we can determine if John is using the word 'love' in the same way as depicted above, or see if he has something different in mind.

---

[74] ἀγαπάω "I love" in Greek. Usually indicates a quality of love that is unselfish and does not depend upon reciprocity from the ones being loved.

Notice, as mentioned above, the use of the conjunction "For." That conjunction does not present the cause of v. 15, in that the one who believes and thus possesses eternal life because of the realities of v. 16. Rather, it explains the meaning of the statement of v. 15 by means of the realities presented in v. 16. That is to say, John 3:16 does not instruct Nicodemus *how* to enter the kingdom. It demonstrates to him whether he already is in or not. Jesus already told Nicodemus how to enter the kingdom in vv. 3-8. The point there is that he has no control over his own entrance into the kingdom whatsoever. He cannot even determine the direction of the wind, let alone determine his own birth. How, then, can he do something as extreme and profound as regeneration?[75]

This fact (man's inability to enter the kingdom) is foundational to John's gospel. We need to review this because there is so much confusion related to who determines entrance into the kingdom.

John began his epistle with the assertion, "But as many as received Him, to them He gave the right to become children of God, even to those who believe in His name, who were born, not of blood nor of the will of the flesh nor of the will of man, but of God" (John 1:12-13). From the beginning, John is teaching his audience that Jesus Christ came to this world, and those who live in this world did not receive Him, specifically the Jews (John 1:11). However, some did "receive" Him. Who were they? They

---

[75] This is what happens when one is born of the water and Spirit, as indicated by Ezekiel 36:25-27.

were those who were born of the will of God (John 1:13b). That is the only way to enter the kingdom of God according to John, and Jesus taught the same.

Later in the book, John records the Lord's instructions to the Galilean crowd which saw Him perform so many miracles since that time at the Passover in Jerusalem (John 4:45; 6:2, 14). This crowd was the kind of crowd that wanted to merely receive benefits from Jesus. So, when it came time for Jesus to ask something from them, they would not give Him what He desired.

It was the end of the discourse in chapter six that the Lord showed them that they had wrong motives for seeking after Him. He declared that they came to see Him not because they were convinced that He is the Messiah, but because they received free food from Him (John 6:26). Then the Lord introduces the reality that the Father has given some to the Son and all of those He gave will come to Him and not perish (John 6:37-40). The conversation escalates as the Lord announces Himself as heavenly sustenance (vv. 41-58). Here we find the Lord introducing the reality that no one is able to come to Him for eternal life unless the Father draws Him to it (v. 44). Jesus is teaching this crowd, this very crowd which observed His miracles at the Passover and the current miracles He was doing in Galilee (John 4:45; 6:2), that they did not believe in Him.

Some may say, "But they had been following Him! They had interrupted their lives for Him! They had done so much to come to see Him! How then could it be that they did not believe?" Well, in today's churches, this activity by the constituency would give most pastors hope that they are true Christians. However, the fact is, external interest does not identify a Christian. The starting point is that a person must be drawn of God. Apart from that, he cannot come to Jesus Christ.

At the end of this narrative, the Lord finally announces to them that it is impossible to come to Christ unless granted to them from the Father (v. 65). Think about it: these disciples had been "faithful" to find Him and went to Him where He was. Yet, almost none of them were actually following Jesus Christ as a result of the drawing work of the Father. Their religious interest and behavior had a completely different source: themselves. It was their own self-interest, not submission to God's will, which drew them. They understood that they simply did not want to buy into what Jesus was saying, because it was too much for them (v. 60). Because of the astounding statement that it is impossible to come to Him unless the Father was drawing them, they turned away from Him and followed Him no more (v. 66). Jesus knew all along who did not believe and who did (v. 64). He identified not so much that some chose to believe and some did not. Rather, He recognized in the hearts of the people (John 2:23-25) to whom faith was given and to whom it was not given.

The next paragraph in this passage is profound. How can we know if someone has eternal life? Again, John 3:15 says that only those who believe possess eternal life. It is only those who believe the Word of God who possess eternal life. Those who do not, just like the multitude who walked away, simply do not possess it and are not drawn to the Son by the Father. However, the twelve were drawn.[76] How do we know? We know because of Peter's admission. He said, "Lord, to whom shall we go? You have words of eternal life. We have believed and have come to know that You are the Holy One of God" (vv. 68-69). They had no alternative. They could not leave Jesus Christ. Why not? Because they believed Him and did not find His Word "too difficult". Thus, they knew that Jesus is the Holy One of God. How did they know? They knew because they had been taught of the Father and drawn to Christ by Him (John 6:45-46).

Finally, there is one more example of this teaching of the Lord that only those who are drawn by God come to Christ (actually, there are many more examples of these, but one more will suffice). In John chapter 10, the Lord is in Jerusalem, but has left the Temple in order to avoid a run-in with the Pharisees. These Pharisees currently wanted to kill Jesus because they thought that He blasphemed when He called Himself the "I AM" of Exodus 3:14 (John 8:58-59). On His way out of the Temple, he heals a man on the Sabbath (John 9:14), who was born blind. In doing so, He broke the traditions of the elders by doing work on the Sabbath. This event was significant because it provided

---

[76] Notice especially what the Lord said later in John. He said, "Did I Myself not choose you, the twelve, and yet one of you is a devil?" (John 6:70). Jesus chose the disciples for service to Him, as well as for eternal life (John 15:16). This is the point of the passage. The absolute will of God, as expressed in whom He would chose for service and eternal life, is the crux of the Gospel.

indisputable proof as to His credentials as Messiah (John 9:30-33). Jesus finds the man, and presents Himself to the man. As a result, the man worships Jesus Christ with a stunning, yet simple statement—"Lord, I believe" (v. 38). This was a simple statement of faith, a faith given to Him at that moment as evidence that the Father was drawing him. Later in this conversation, Jesus teaches that the sheep hear the voice of the true Shepherd and, upon hearing His voice, they follow Him. Who are these sheep? Another conversation later in the season tells us.

In John 10:22-42, Jesus is disputing with the Jews concerning whether or not He is the Christ (v. 24). He tells them plainly, "I told you and you do not believe" (v. 25). Notice that it is not so much that they *did not* believe, in time past, but that they currently, at the time of this conversation, *do not* believe. This is an indication that they are not being drawn of the Father, and did not possess eternal life. Why did they not believe? Is it because they were simply not interested? No, we know that is not why because they had "asked" of Him proof as to His messiahship. Is it because Jesus' teaching was unclear? No, we know that is not why because He says that He told them plainly and showed many good works as proof (vv. 25, 32). Then what drove their unbelief? It was this: they were never God's sheep. Jesus said, "You do not believe because you are not of My sheep" (v. 26). Notice that He did not say, "You are not of My sheep because you do not believe." Their belief in Christ was predicated by whether or not they were *already* His sheep. Did they choose to be His sheep? No. That decision was made by the Father because v. 29 indicates that the Father gave them (the sheep) to the Son. When did that happen? It certainly wasn't impromptu in front of Christ. The indication in all of this is that the Father predetermined those He would create for the Son and that, upon hearing His voice, they would come to the Son. Thus, Jesus asserts, "All that the Father gives to Me will come to Me, and the one who comes to Me I will certainly not cast out" (John 6:37).

Folks, understand that God has predetermined, by His own will, unmoved by the behavior of anyone, to create some people for the Son. The Son came to redeem them, and return them to Himself forever and they will never perish. All of this is the plan of God, and is in no way of man.

John surely wants us to understand by the Lord's own teaching that the choice in salvation is not ours, but God's. In order to believe, *you must already be His sheep.* In order to be a sheep of Christ's, *you must have been predestined to be such by the Father.* Those who do not believe are full demonstration that they lack eternal life. They are unregenerate. Those who lack eternal life never demonstrate belief in Christ and are not His sheep.[77]

---

[77] Yet, this does not mean that we are free to condemn people. We cannot know if at some point in the future they might repent. If we "nail them to the wall," so to speak, as to the apparent fact that they are not saved, we have lost our opportunity to possibly see them come to Christ. The most exciting thing I can think of, outside of seeing Jesus Christ face to face, is to witness the regeneration of a sinner before my very eyes!

As we continue to examine John 3:16, I want to reiterate the fact that v. 16 is nothing more than an explanation of the assertion of v. 15.[78] Those who possess belief in Christ demonstrate that they possess eternal life. That is to say, only those who possess faith in Jesus Christ will possess eternal life and not those who do not believe in Him. With this understanding, the intent and meaning of v. 16 becomes apparent. Further, understanding this informs us as to the love that Jesus speaks of here. The love of God is demonstrated to the world and the extent of it is the rescuing of those who would believe, His people (Matthew 1:21), so that they would not perish. This is the ministry of the Lord: He came to seek and to save "the lost" (Luke 19:10). However, not everyone who is a sinner is lost. Rather, only those who were sovereignly predestined to be "sheep," and are unsaved, are lost. Jesus said, "I have other sheep, which are not of this fold; I must bring them also, and they will hear my voice; and they will become one flock with one shepherd" (John 10:16). Jesus teaches that the plan of God was that there were some who were already sheep and yet have not heard of Him, apart from the fold of Israel (Isaiah 56:6-8), and those who are of Israel who are sheep as well. Again, not every sinner is a lost sheep. In fact, the judgment of the Lord, wherein He separates the sheep from the goats, is that

---

[78] It must also be seen that v. 15 is a further explanation of vv. 13-14. We can see this because of the particle of v. 15, "so that." That is stating the purpose of the statement coming from v. 14 which indicates that in the same manner that the serpent was lifted upon the pole, so much also the Son of Man be lifted up. Further, the "Son of Man" is He who descended from heaven to this earth (v. 13). So, as we see, this is a very tight argument from our Lord concerning immense truths about His kingdom.

separation of those who were created as sheep and those who were never sheep to begin with (Matthew 25:31-46). It is said of the sheep, "'Come, you who are blessed of My Father, inherit the kingdom prepared for you from the foundation of the world" (V. 34). The "sheep" have had the kingdom prepared for them from the foundation of the world. That kingdom was not prepared for the goats.[79] But, the question comes, "How do we know who is a sheep or a goat?" That is the point of John 3:15-16. Only those who will believe are sheep. Those who will never believe are goats. In other words, only those whom God has given to the Son, and created to be such, will inherit eternal life because only those who are "sheep" will ever believe. Those who continue to refuse Jesus Christ, refuse to believe His words, refuse to obey His command to repent, they are goats and will not inherit the kingdom, since it was not prepared for them.

Yet there is more to consider here concerning the love of God. Our English translations seem to indicate that God loves the world. We read that and we think that God has good feelings for the world, despite their utter hatred of Him. We think it is awful nice of God to provide a way of salvation for everybody in the death of His Son. However, that is not the case in this verse. God

---

[79] What is prepared for them is spoken of in v. 41. The eternal fire is that fire that is prepared for the devil and his angels, his emissaries. Those who are "sons of the evil one" (Matthew 13:38) will follow their "father" (John 8:44) into that fire. Thus, the kingdom is not prepared for everyone, only for whom God Himself has elected and predestined.

does not love the world in the manner often thought of in this verse.[80] Let me explain.

Remember, John 3:16 is an explanation for v. 15. Verse 15 teaches that only those who believe in Christ will possess eternal life. It is not that just anyone will possess eternal life. It is reserved for only those who believe. However, only those with eternal life believe. Verse 15 indicates that those who believe demonstrate that they have eternal life. The next question, then, would be, "How do they get eternal life?" That question is answered in v. 16

God's love brought His eternal plan (Ephesians 3:11) into history. God "demonstrated" his love to the world in a certain way. The verse begins with an adverb that indicates that there was a manner in which love was demonstrated.[81] There was a way in which God's love, in the past, was demonstrated. Realize that the word "love" is not a future-tense verb. It does not say, "For God will love the world..." Nicodemus is being told that God

---

[80] Consider James 4:4, "You adulteresses, do you not know that friendship with the world is hostility toward God? Therefore whoever wishes to be a friend of the world makes himself an enemy of God." Also consider 1 John 2:15 "Do not love the world nor the things in the world. If anyone loves the world, the love of the Father is not in him." These instructions from these men teach us that love for the world is inconsistent with the love of God. We are never called to love the world. We are only called to *demonstrate* love *to* the world. There is a very big difference between the two. God is not on friendly terms with the world, nor the world with God.
[81] See Gundry, Robert H., and Russell W. Howell. 1999. "The Sense and Syntax of John 3:14-17 with Special Reference to the Use of OYTŌS...ŌSTE in John 3:16." *Novum Testamentum* 41, no. 1: 24-39. *ATLASerials, Religion Collection*, EBSCO*host* (accessed January 15, 2014).

loved in some manner in time past in relation to himself. Since the cross is still future, the love of God demonstrated to the world is not necessarily the cross, although it includes it. The verse tells you what it is that demonstrates God's love-He gave His Only-Begotten Son. The giving of His Son was a demonstration of the manner of God's love to the world. Again, what is not being said here is "God is in love with the world." There is no indication that God has good feelings for the world in the way that we might have pity on a homeless man. The sentimentalism involved in that cannot be transferred to the God of heaven. He has disdain for the world. He despises our waywardness and cannot stand our rebellion. Psalm 7 encapsulates this reality very well. David wrote in Psalm 7:10–16

> *"My shield is with God,*
> *Who saves the upright in heart.*
> *God is a righteous judge,*
> *And a God who has indignation every day.*
> *If a man does not repent, He will sharpen His sword;*
> *He has bent His bow and made it ready.*
> *He has also prepared for Himself deadly weapons;*
> *He makes His arrows fiery shafts.*
> *Behold, he travails with wickedness,*
> *And he conceives mischief and brings forth falsehood.*
> *He has dug a pit and hollowed it out,*
> *And has fallen into the hole which he made.*
> *His mischief will return upon his own head,*
> *And his violence will descend upon his own pate."*

In this Psalm, David writes concerning how God must feel concerning the wicked, in this case a man. This man is unknown historically, but apparently was one that pursued David vehemently. However, what is said in this Psalm concerning the way God feels about the wicked is the consistent impression throughout Scripture.[82] Yet, because God is love (1 John 4:8), He does not take pleasure in the death of the wicked (Ezekiel 18:32). He does not enjoy it when the wicked must be punished for their calamities against God. Nevertheless, His justice demands it.

The indication of Psalm 5:4-6 is that God indeed hates the sinner, those who love iniquity. David wrote,

> *"For You are not a God who takes pleasure in wickedness;*
> *No evil dwells with You.*
> *The boastful shall not stand before Your eyes;*
> *You hate all who do iniquity.*
> *You destroy those who speak falsehood;*
> *The Lord abhors the man of bloodshed and deceit."*

An emotional love that is filled with man-centered pity is not the love of God as portrayed in John 3:16. The love that is portrayed in John 3:16 is a love that is demonstrated to a world that hates God and loves darkness (John 3:19[83]) in order to reprove them. He gives manifold demonstrations of His love to the world. He has, and continues, to bear witness of His great love to the world. This love is the righteousness that men suppress. It is in view in Romans 1:18-32 wherein Paul instructs us that God, although known within man, i.e. his conscience, is

---

[82] Consider Exodus 15:1-16; Psalms 94:23; 97; Romans 3:9-18; Revelation 19:11-21

[83] Notice that in John 3:19 the word "world" is equated with "men" later in the same verse. This is consistently the sense of the word throughout John.

suppressed by the unrighteous deeds of sin. The reality of God's love is there and the knowledge of His love is suppressed by men by hate-filled actions as described in vv. 24-32.

Paul teaches us this in his speech to the idolatrous Lycaonians. In Acts 14:12-18, Paul attempts to restrain the people from worshiping him and his companions because they had healed a lame man. First he tells them that they are men like the Lycaonians and do not deserve to be worshiped. Then Paul introduces them to the God of creation. The scene is amazing. They want to sacrifice to them, demonstrating their pagan ways (v. 13). Barnabas and Paul rushed out into the crowd and confronted them telling that they should turn to the true God. Who is this God? He is the One who "...did not leave Himself without witness, in that He did good and gave you rains from heaven and fruitful seasons, satisfying your hearts with food and gladness" (Vv. 16-17). God's witness to Himself was His giving of good things, including food and drink in abundance. This is the love God has for the world: love which provides good things to others, even to one's enemies (Luke 6:27; Romans 12:21; Galatians 6:10). That is the sense of John 3:16, for God does not love the world in the sense of emotional, sentimental endorsement of it in and of itself. The flood shows us how God feels about the world (Genesis 6:5-6), and we are worse than the Antediluvian world that God destroyed.

So, how did God love the world? Simple, He loved the world the same way He has always shown love to the world—by providing care for it. By patiently overlooking the ignorance, willful as it is, of men in times past. Everything that man has he has received from God (Psalm 104). All the food, clothing, and pleasure are the direct result of the kindness and love of YHWH. Even the most vile of human beings has sunshine and a good meal at his disposal (Acts 14:16-17). This is the love of God. He, by doing this, leaves Himself "a witness" (Acts 14:16). He testifies by His kindness, which is supposed to lead people to repentance (Romans 2:4; cf. 1:18-20), of the fact that He is holy and good and man is not. True to man's nature, however, they refuse Him who is speaking (Hebrews 12:25). God provides for them all their needs. Yet, although He has loved them, they deny Him and refuse to give Him glory (Romans 3:23). The testimony of His love, regardless of the condition of men's hearts, by the sending of His Son into this world is in view in John 3:16. This is not a love bestowed upon man because of man. This is a love demonstrated to man regardless of man's will and condition. It is simply that God is love and He was demonstrating that love to the world.

In fact, the most extreme testimony to God's love is the death of His beloved Son, Jesus Christ. God's greatest act of love for His Son, and the Son for the Father (John 14:31), was demonstrated to the world by lifting Christ up on the cross for the entire world to see.

"that He gave His only-begotten Son…"

Psalm 2:7 says,

> *"I will surely tell of the decree of the Lord:*
> *He said to Me, 'You are My Son,*
> *Today I have begotten You.'"*

Jesus uses this phrase, "Only-Begotten Son" from Psalm 2. Who is this Son? He is the One who will receive from the Father the nations and the earth, which is the kingdom. Moreover, this Son is the only-begotten one in a very peculiar and unique way.

This verse is referred to three times in the New Testament (see Acts 13:33; Hebrews 1:5; 5:5) although the concept of "begotten" is reiterated seven times, including the above verses (see John 1:14, 18; 3:18; 1 John 4:9). Jesus Christ is the Only-Begotten One of the Father. Yet, what does that mean? It does not refer to His incarnation. We know that because that is never the sense of it in the other three uses of the passage in the New Testament. Instead, this is used most often in reference to the Lord's resurrection from the dead. Peter understood it that way in Acts 13:33, saying that Jesus has been raised from the dead as it says in the Second Psalm. That Psalm, as interpreted by Peter (and thus the Holy Spirit), refers to the resurrection of Jesus Christ, not His incarnation. Paul also alludes to this very thing, although not using the second Psalm as his reference. He wrote in Romans 6:4 that Jesus Christ was raised unto "newness of life." Therefore, Christ was given life and *that* is the sense of "begotten" in Psalm 2. This is not to say that He was spiritually dead in the previous years to His resurrection. Rather, in His death He conquered death and was brought back to eternal, glorified life by means of the resurrection. That resurrection, then, became the declaration of His Sonship, as Paul taught in Romans 1:1-4.

The astounding thing is, God the Father *gave Him over* to us![84] This Man to whom Nicodemus is speaking is the Son who is the only-begotten of the Father who was sent to the earth. I believe that Nicodemus was introduced to this truth that night as He spoke with Jesus, but it was not until later that this reality hit him.

God gave His Son over to the world that valued darkness over light (John 3:19). He presented His Son to the world as a demonstration of His love. That is not to say that He loved the world in the same way that He loves His Son. God is love and demonstrated this love by giving His Son to enter the World. To give the Son is to present Him to the world. Remember, the Son is the Heir of the world. John tells us, "He came to His own and those who were His own received Him not" (John 1:11). This world is His world by means of creation. The people in this world are either sons of the kingdom or sons of the evil one. Christ came to this world to rescue the sons of God from the tyranny of the evil one (Hebrews 2:14). Yet it is important to note that this mission was both a rescue operation and a judgment. How so? The same world which He entered is the same world which killed Him. However, within that world, are those who are also sheep,

---

[84] He was given as life to some, and judgment to others, as will be understood in the following. This is not the sentiment of loving the world more than His Son. His love of His Son is extended to the world for their observation and repentance.

chosen of the Father for the Son. A good illustration of this fact is in the salvation of 3,000 souls on Pentecost (Acts 2:41). Just fifty days prior, these were the same people, led by the apostate and godless religious leaders of Judaism, the Pharisees, who cried for Christ's crucifixion (Matthew 27:20-26). However, even in doing that, they were still sheep. They were God's people. Some will ask, "How could they have done what they did then?" To ask that indicates a basic ignorance concerning the depth of our depravity.

"that whoever believes in Him shall not perish, but have eternal life."

This last segment of John 3:16 finishes the thought of the previous section of the verse. We have seen that God demonstrated His love to the world by giving His Only-Begotten Son to the world. Why did He do that? John answers that the reason is that God's plan is to rescue the sons of God from death. Remember, it was for the sons of the kingdom that He prepared the kingdom. However, the sons of the kingdom were subject to death by the trickery of Satan and the disobedience of Adam. God followed through with His promise of death for Adam's disobedience and subjected the entire human race to death (Genesis 2:15-17; 3:19; Romans 5:12). It would seem that Satan, then, was the victor. By his trickery, he "forced" God's hand to kill the very sons whom He had created as brethren for the Son. However, the gospel is focused upon redemption. This redemption is an act of the power of God to retrieve God's people back to Himself, past the confines of death and the curse.[85] In this way God's original design and plan resulting in many sons in the kingdom of His Son would be accomplished.[86] Jesus said, "My sheep hear My voice, and I know them, and they follow Me; and I give eternal life to them, and they will never perish; and no one will snatch them out of My hand" (John 10:27-28). All of this is the plan of God.

Retrieving those who believe in Jesus Christ, which is the result of eternal life, is the act of God whereby perishing is no longer an option. To understand the depth and sense of this magnificent thought, we must understand "perishing."

The word for "perish" is the Greek word referring to something coming to ruin, or being destroyed.[87] It is a strong word that indicates a kind of death that comes by means of utter destruction. It is not simply ceasing to exist, but that of a forced-upon destruction from an outside source.[88] To perish is to be

---

[85] In Galatians 3:13-14 Paul identifies the fact that the curse is from the failure to obey the Law of Moses. The punishment for disobedience in the garden was not a curse, but a simple punishment. Paul wrote that it was not until the Law came which centuries after Adam, that a curse was imputed upon man (Romans 5:12-14).

[86] The sonship of believers is the goal of redemption. Given the magnanimity of such a topic, it will be the subject matter of a future book. For now, one must consider the use of the term "son(s)" so very often in Romans 8 in relation to the Eschaton (cf. Revelation 21:7).
[87] ἀπόλλυμι *apollymi* destroy; lose; die; be lost" Horst Robert Balz and Gerhard Schneider, vol. 1, *Exegetical Dictionary of the New Testament* (Grand Rapids, Mich.: Eerdmans, 1990-), 135.

[88] In contrast to σῴζεσθαι or to ζωὴ αἰώνιος, ἀπόλλυσθαι is definitive destruction, not merely in the sense of the extinction of physical

subject to eternal damnation at the hands of God. Remember, God condemned man in his rebellion. The physical death that comes to all men is the first step in the perishing. The second step, which has not yet occurred, is the judgment seat of the Father (Revelation 20:11-15).

Specifically, perishing has to do with eternal death. It is, as was said before, that absolute death that occurs by means of God's judgment on the sinner. This is unthinkable for the sons of the kingdom. For them to perish in the manner that the wicked do is simply inconsistent with God's plan and is the focus and effort of Satan from the beginning. Jesus said that Satan was a murderer from the beginning (John 8:44), and Peter says that Satan prowls about like a roaring lion seeking someone to devour (1 Peter 5:8). Satan has shown himself to be a murderer from the creation of the world. But of all his murders, none are more heinous than when he filled the heart of his servant, Judas, and had Jesus betrayed, arrested, and killed on the cross (John 13:27). That act alone revealed more about Satan than all of his other acts combined. His wicked heart, perverse mind, and diabolical will were all focused upon the destruction of the Son of God.

---

existence, but rather of an eternal plunge into Hades and a hopeless destiny of death in the depiction of which such terms as ὀργή, θυμός, θλῖψις and στενοχωρία are used (R. 2:8 f.) , *Theological Dictionary of the New Testament*, ed. Gerhard Kittel, Geoffrey W. Bromiley and Gerhard Friedrich, vol. 1, electronic ed. (Grand Rapids, MI: Eerdmans, 1964-), 396.

What is important to realize is that Satan is not responsible for taking the life of anyone. Rather, God is. God is responsible for the destruction of sinners. Consider these passages:

In reference to the flood,

The Lord said, "I will blot out man whom I have created from the face of the land, from man to animals to creeping things and to birds of the sky; for I am sorry that I have made them." (Genesis 6:7)

In reference to Israel's rebellion and apostasy,

"It shall come about that as the Lord delighted over you to prosper you, and multiply you, so the Lord will delight over you to make you perish and destroy you; and you will be torn from the land where you are entering to possess it" (Deuteronomy 28:63).

Then I saw a great white throne and Him who sat upon it, from whose presence earth and heaven fled away, and no place was found for them. And I saw the dead, the great and the small, standing before the throne, and books were opened; and another book was opened, which is the book of life; and the dead were judged from the things which were written in the books, according to their deeds. And the sea gave up the dead which were in it, and death and Hades gave up the dead which were in them; and they were judged, every one of them according to their deeds. Then death and Hades were thrown into the lake of fire. This is the second death, the lake of fire. And if anyone's name was not found written in the book of life, he was thrown into the lake of fire" (Revelation 20:11–15).

These few passages refer to extreme calamity in the lives of those receiving God's judgment. However, you never see God apologize for His actions. His punishment of sin is just. Those who perish, by the hand of God Himself, are the unbelieving and non-receiving ones. These people demonstrate that they are not God's sheep, and thus must perish. The perishing of these wicked persons will be facilitated by the angels who do God's bidding (Matthew 13:49-50). These angels will be sent out into the kingdom and they will gather the wicked together and bring them before the throne of Christ. Jesus Christ will then pronounce judgment upon them for their deeds and from that judgment they will eventually be cast into the lake of fire at the final judgment of God the Father (Revelation 20:11-15).

The question might come, "Who are the wicked?" To answer, the wicked are all those whose nature and heart are dark and full of unrighteousness. John wrote years later about this very question.

"Little children, make sure no one deceives you; the one who practices righteousness is righteous, just as He is righteous; the one who practices sin is of the devil; for the devil has sinned from the beginning. The Son of God appeared for this purpose, to destroy the works of the devil. No one who is born of God practices sin, because His seed abides in him; and he cannot sin, because he is born of God. By this the children of God and the children of the devil are obvious: anyone who does not practice righteousness is not of God, nor the one who does not love his brother." (1 John 3:7-10)

"But aren't all people like that? Doesn't that describe the condition of everyone?" Yes. It does. That is what makes salvation that much more incredible. Paul wrote to the Galatians, "But the Scripture has shut up everyone under sin, so that the promise by faith in Jesus Christ might be given to those who believe" (Galatians 3:22). Every person has been bitten by the serpent, so to speak, and is perishing. How is anyone saved then? And that is the question one must produce in order to escape the perishing that is inevitable. That is the question that Nicodemus must ask as well, and he ultimately did.

It is the display of this love from the Father that draws men to Jesus Christ (John 12:32). Paul taught that the cross was the demonstration of righteousness to the world (Romans 3:21-26). The cross upon which the Son of God died demonstrates a kind of righteousness that the Law could never demonstrate, although being testified to by the Law. God's judgment upon His Son because of sins He did not commit, and yet were placed upon Him by the Father, displays the unbending righteousness of God.

The glorious work of the Lord Jesus Christ is that He came to this earth in order to rescue His flock from the tyranny and power of death. That rescue is the heart and soul of every discussion the Lord had with people. In fact, it is the heart and soul of the Lord's discussion with Nicodemus that night. Nicodemus would later prove to be one that would believe and have eternal life. He was God's child, God's sheep, from before the foundation of the world (Ephesians 1:5). However, Nicodemus did not understand that. His heart was hard, his mind was dark, and his self-righteousness was pervasive. But God, in His power, transcended that and rescued him from death. That is the gospel and the message of John 3:16. Because of the Son's submission to this plan of the Father, Christ could rightly say that of all that the Father has given Him, He lost not one (John 6:39; 18:9).

THE IMPLICATIONS

We have endeavored to explain John 3:16 in such a way that it makes sense to the reader by breaking this verse into parts. Because of the emotion attached to this verse, to see this verse in any way aside from the popular interpretation, even if one presents the accurate interpretation, is potentially volatile to some readers. However, it should be the purpose and goal of every Christian to simply understand the text of Scripture with clarity, unmixed by previous incorrect understandings of a text. In reality, we should come to a passage of Scripture as if we have never studied it before and discover all over again what it is teaching.

If we are to summarize John 3:16, we would summarize it like this: Only those who believe possess eternal life, only the sheep of God will believe, and their belief evidences the eternal life which God gives them by means of the hearing of the Word of Christ (Romans 10:17). Because they believe and possess eternal life, the Son's righteousness is given to them (imputation) for their salvation, thus avoiding eternal damnation at the hand of the Father. At the heart of this is the wonderful fact that God loves. As a demonstration of His love, for the Son and the sheep,

He sent His Son to the earth to be born of a virgin. This way He would live, die, and be resurrected just like His brethren. Sadly, the darkened world despises the Son of God and will never come to Him of their own accord. It is impossible for them to come because they, by nature, don't want to. However, some will come by means of hearing the gospel and being given faith to repent and believe, all through the sovereign will of God. All of the above is the manner in which God demonstrated love to the world.

What our Lord is teaching Nicodemus is that he is in an impossible spot. He is being forced to ask some hard questions: "Do I believe? Do I have eternal life?" If he does not, he now knows that he cannot enter the kingdom. I think that the terror of this thinking struck him hard. Thankfully, as verse 17 states, "God did not send the Son into the world to judge the world, but that the world might be saved through him." I would imagine that Nicodemus was glad to hear this. Had Jesus come to judge, Nicodemus knew that he would have been judged on the spot, spending an eternity in eternal fire. However, Jesus came to "save the world." Again, as proven above, that cannot mean that everyone alive would be, or could be, saved. "The world" refers to the location of people in the world. Some of those in the world will be saved by Jesus Christ, whereas others won't. However, the intent of the Father was to send the Son to announce salvation before judgment. Only those who believe in Him are not judged (v. 18). He who does not believe evidences the fact that judgment resides upon that man already. Why? Because he does not believe in the name of the Only-Begotten Son of God. If a person does believe, that would evidence eternal life. The realities contained in this passage are stunning, to say the least! In Moses' day, when the people were complaining, God sent serpents to punish some by causing them to be bitten and thus perish. Once the people acknowledged the fact that they had sinned, they cried out to Moses and God confessing their sins. God then instructed Moses to make a replica on a pole of the snakes that were biting people. In doing so, if the people would look toward the serpent placed upon the top of the pole, they would be rescued from death. The reality is however, none of them would have looked if it were not for God's gracious will *causing* them to look.

In the same way, Jesus Christ, the Only-Begotten Son of God, was placed upon a cross in order that those who look to Him in faith will be rescued from the death of the judgment seat of God. *The sending of the Son to satisfy the Father and to be a substitute for the sheep is the love of God demonstrated to the world.* This is greater than any gift of sustenance God has ever given to man. Yet, as with the other provisions, the giving of the Son is simply a testimony to the world of the love of God. The sad and damning fact is that the world hates God and is at enmity with Him. Therefore, in order to rescue the sons of the kingdom, He must allow His Son to endure the "rage of the nations" (Psalm 2:1-3; cf. Acts 4:25-28), and He most certainly endured. Yet He did it not for His own sake, He did it for the joy that was set before Him (Hebrews 12:1-2). What joy was that? It was the joy of loving reunion with the Father and the accomplishment of all that the Father commanded Him. After His resurrection, Jesus Christ sat down at the right hand of the Father (Psalm 110:1). In doing so, He was given back the glory that was His from eternity. Now He is Lord and He will one day assume lordship over this planet as the God-Man (Zechariah 14:1ff.; cf. Philippians 2:9-11).

But, the implication of understanding John 3:16 is that only those who are predestined to believe, as determined by the will of the Father and not by the people themselves, will inherit eternal life. *Eternal life is not for everyone. It is only for those for whom the kingdom has been prepared from the foundation of the world.* This is extremely offensive to many, as it should be.

The Offense

Why would anyone be offended at the thought that God will only save those whom He has chosen? After all, men loved darkness rather than light anyway. It is not as if they want to be saved. The free will of God to save those whom he has already chosen offends many, even Christians, because they have no control over their salvation. The idea that we cannot contribute to our salvation according to *our* own "free will" offends our pride. Men have always understood and been taught that they can have anything they want if they work hard enough for it.

However, in the case of the kingdom of God, salvation is not theirs to attain. The fact is, only those who are written in the Lamb's book of life will inherit eternal life (Revelation 20:15). Nothing a person can do can earn him the right to be written in that book. Therefore, you are completely helpless, and yet happy in your twisted, depraved helplessness. This is what causes offense to many.

Let's look at this more because it is crucial to the world's response to the gospel. Too many Christians and pastors look at John 3:16 as a statement concerning how to enter the kingdom. By that, I mean that they consider John 3:16 as a formula for entrance. However, as we saw, it is only an explanation of the reason why one who believes possesses eternal life. Why does one who believes in Jesus Christ possess eternal life? Because, Jesus Christ, the Only-Begotten Son, was lifted up for all men to look towards and those who received eternal life did look toward Him by the drawing work of the Father. Only those who are made to look toward Him by the work of the Father possesses eternal life. Their believing demonstrates the eternal life they possess.

But what about those who "look" but don't appear to have eternal life? Or, what about those who don't look to Him? How does that work?

One aspect of the ministry of Jesus Christ was also to judge. I realize that Jesus said that He did not come into this world to judge the world. However, He did say that it was for judgment that He came into this world. There is a judgment coming. There is a day in which God will judge the secrets of men's hearts by one Man, Jesus Christ (Romans 2:14-16; cf. Acts 17:30-31). That judgment is sure and is coming. With that in mind, every conversation Jesus had with people either relieved that person from judgment, or confirmed them in it. He was a Savior to some, and a Judge to others. What is the basis of this distinction? The basis of this distinction was whether or not they could "see."

Seeing and Hearing

The Apostle John wrote about an incident in the ninth chapter of his gospel that demonstrates this reality and does so in vivid terms. John recalls a time when Jesus had healed a grown man who was born blind. This man was located by Christ in the inquisition of His disciples about God's justice (John 9:1-2). The reality was, this man was chosen from before the foundation of the world to display the glory of God (v. 3). These works displayed in this man refer to the works of Messiah, which he was predestined to display. Unwittingly, all the long years of having no sight, and the disdain of his parents, were all for that one moment wherein Jesus would walk by and heal him, demonstrating His authority over blindness.

The Serpent and the Cross

The crux of the matter was not the healing of a man, but that Jesus did such on the Sabbath. John tells us, "Now it was a Sabbath on the day when Jesus made the clay and opened his eyes" (John 9:14). This piece of information tells us of the hypocrisy and self-righteousness of these religious leaders of Israel. They did not care that a man was given sight after years of sightlessness. They were more concerned that Jesus follow their prescriptions of Sabbath observance, prescriptions not taught in Torah. These Pharisees demonstrate the true blindness, and the blind man's true vision. After healing the man, he appeared before the Pharisees for their evaluation. Some said that this healing was sinful because it was done on the Sabbath. Some were more concerned about the fact that this miracle occurred, Sabbath notwithstanding (v. 16). In general, they did not believe that this man was born blind. They called the parents of the man in and interrogated them. What was the parent's response? Out of fear for the Jews, they said "He is of age, ask him" (vv. 20-23). Why did they confirm him as their son, and yet refused to take the discussion further? Because they knew that if they agreed that Jesus did the miracle, they would be kicked out of the synagogue and they could not bear that thought. They were willing to allow their grown son to be put out of the synagogue instead of them. The man is interrogated, he finds it amazing that the Pharisees can't understand the fact that Jesus did this miracle and that they do not know how to judge the situation. They become upset with him and put him out of the synagogue (v. 34). Jesus finds the man, again, and asked him if he believed in the

Son of Man. He asked who the Son of Man is, and Jesus revealed Himself to him. The man's reply was, "'Lord, I believe.' And he worshiped Him" (v. 38). The reply from the Lord is "For judgment I came into this world, so that those who do not see may see, and those who see may become blind" (v. 39).

This profound statement encapsulates the Lord's ministry to the world. It is that those who are blind may see and those who see may become blind. This is related to judgment in the sense that the seeing or blind condition of man determines the result of judgment when Christ, the Judge, rules in the time to come. Thus, He came to sort out, as it were, those who see and those who don't. But, what does that mean? In short, those who are blind but eventually see must be related to those who, like this man in the narrative, do not have physical, or spiritual, sight (and know it) but gain both. However, those who have physical sight and *think* they have spiritual sight (and don't know it) have neither. The blind man made seeing will enter eternal life. The "seeing" Pharisees truly blind will enter eternal damnation.[89] This ministry of our Lord was not only to call the sinners to repentance, but to call specific sinners to repentance. The sinners that He targeted were the "sheep," the "blind," and the "deaf." These are the poor in spirit who will inherit the kingdom

---

[89]"Seeing" and "hearing" have an extensive use in the Scriptures. Most notably the Lord speaks of the judgment upon the Jews, the religious leaders of Israel, as being deaf and blind (Matthew 13:14-15; cp. Isaiah 6:9-10). It has been their habit to be such since the days of the Prophet Isaiah. They did not see their blindness so as to see clearly. They did not hear their own deafness so as to hear the Word of the Lord. The Jews of Jesus' day were of the same quality-blind and deaf to their one depravity and God's Word.

of God (Matthew 5:3). They are those who, once they hear the voice of the Great Shepherd, they will follow. They really don't have a choice. It may, as in the case of Nicodemus, represent a struggle as he counts the cost of such a decision. However, they will eventually be given eternal life, submit to Christ, and do so with a grateful heart, all by the power of God.

It might be seen that Jesus was calling everyone on the planet to Himself and they would have to decide whether or not they would follow. However, the truth is He *was* calling the entire planet to Himself. Yet, only those who were blind, and knew it, were given sight. To those blind, and did not know it, they were confined in their blindness. That is the gospel of Jesus Christ and it is dependent upon the fact that not everyone will inherit the kingdom of God. Only those for whom it has been prepared will enter.

The Apostle Paul also explains this reality in his own ministry. He wrote,

"But thanks be to God, who always leads us in triumph in Christ, and manifests through us the sweet aroma of the knowledge of Him in every place. For we are a fragrance of Christ to God among those who are being saved and among those who are perishing; to the one an aroma from death to death, to the other an aroma from life to life. And who is adequate for these things? For we are not like many, peddling the word of God, but as

from sincerity, but as from God, we speak in Christ in the sight of God." (2 Corinthians 2:14–17)

Paul was a preacher. He announced the gospel of Jesus Christ. He announced the very same gospel that Jesus Himself announced. There is no other gospel (Galatians 1:6-9). Therefore, since the gospel that Jesus preached was one that depended upon the dynamics of deafness and blindness, then so also did Paul's gospel as well. However, he used different terms, at least with the Corinthian church. He said that everywhere he went, his preaching manifested the sweet aroma of the knowledge of Christ in every place. Paul and his companions were a fragrant aroma of Christ to God. But notice that these servants and their message were a fragrant aroma to God about Christ whether it referred to those being saved, or those who are perishing. They, those being saved and those perishing, hear the same message. They see the same messenger. They are called upon to do the same things-repent and believe. Yet, to one, it produces life. To the other, death. Both outcomes are still acceptable to God the Father.

He also mentions that to the one perishing, the gospel Paul preached was "from death to death." That means that they, being in a condition of death, spiritual death, continue in that condition and as a result of their refusal to repent, they are confirmed in that condition. However, for those who are being saved, they go from "life to life." What is curious about these designations is that the categories that these people start from are described as "death" and "life." Knowing that all men are dead in their trespasses and sins, how is it that some are described as "life"? The only answer is that these are the categories of those to whom he is preaching as determined by God. In other words, they who are dead are the sons of the evil one (Matthew 13:38) and they who are alive are the sons of the kingdom (Matthew 13:38). The sons of the evil one are not predestined for salvation. They are tares among the field of wheat. Those who are the sons of the kingdom can be defined as alive in the sense that they are destined for life by the Father's creation of them and their predetermined election by Him.[90]

This distinction is the same one the Lord Himself faced as He entered the world to call all men to Himself. Yet, the reality is,

---

[90] This is explained further by the terms "Book of Life" we see on the Old and New Testaments. The Book of Life is that "listing" of the names of those who were originally designed by God to be created and "given" to the Son as a gift. Although it would appear that names are erased from the Book of Life, the reality remains that those who names are written there are those who are registered to be given to the Lamb, thus the Lamb's Book of Life (Revelation 13:8; 21:27). The writing of such names occurred prior to the foundation of the world (Revelation 17:8). To be erased from this book would mean a loss of predestination as the Lamb's possession. However, there are clearly other books in which names and deeds are written (Revelation 20:12; cf. Daniel 7:10) from which men will be judged. It is only those who have been written in the singular book of the Lamb, the Book of Life, who will inherit the kingdom (Luke 10:10). It would appear that the names of those who inherit eternal life were written there before the foundation of the world, and remained there as those who would inherit the kingdom. Thus, any threat of blotting out of the book was real (Exodus 32:32; Psalm 49:28; Revelation 3:5), yet, in God's preserving purpose for those chosen of God for Christ, their names would remain. This only serves to heighten the level of God's absolute will and power in the plan for redemption for those whom He has predestined for the Son. This is an immense reality and rarely considered, but must be.

only those predetermined to life will come. The rest will reject and remain hardened in their dead sins (Ephesians 2:1-10). This is also the reality that Luke wrote about in Acts 13:48; "When the Gentiles heard this, they began rejoicing and glorifying the word of the Lord; *and as many as had been appointed to eternal life believed*" (Emphasis mine). They were not appointed to eternal life *at the time of their belief*. They were appointed to eternal life *before* they believed and *that* alone determined whether they would believe. Unless a person comprehends and believes these things, his ministry to the Lord will be something other than the ministry that the Lord Himself accomplished.[91]

---

[91] See also Acts 2:37-39.

Chapter 8

WHATEVER HAPPENED TO NICODEMUS?

Nicodemus had a lot to consider that evening. This Pharisee of Pharisees came to Jesus to flatter and potentially trap Him in something He might say. Yet he was altogether unsuccessful, being trapped himself. It was his ignorance, coupled by an unclean conscience, which caused him to fail. All of his efforts, as sincere as they may have been, were useless for gaining entrance to the kingdom of God. In fact, he did not even understand what entrance to the kingdom meant. His ignorance was absolutely astounding, and I would have to agree with the Lord and ask, "Are you the teacher of Israel and you do not understand these things?" (John 3:10).

In many ways, Nicodemus-like people are alive and well in the church. Sadly, they even preach Sunday after Sunday in the pulpits of numerous churches. They are those who, although capable of doing so, do not understand the realities of the kingdom, salvation, nor the gospel. They are in a position of darkness that is compounded by false knowledge. In other words, they have sincerity, but completely lack accuracy in their doctrine. The result of this is an unclean conscience. This conscience is one that still loves darkness and refuses the light, leading to eternal judgment. Far too many Christians and pastors have traded in *knowledge* of the Word of God for *feelings* about the Word of God. In doing so, we have established an entirely new set of definitions for biblical terms such as grace, faith, atonement, church, and the gospel. We have exchanged biblical definitions of these terms for definitions that make the greatest number of unbelievers satisfied and content in their ignorance.

The emptiness of our definitions is horrifying. To us, faith is an emotional attachment to an ideal, grace is mere freedom from rules, atonement was a nice idea for the ancients but not for modernity, the church exists for the unbeliever, and the gospel restores your self-esteem. The realities of the kingdom for far too many Christians are close to fairy-tale myths and wishful thinking. After all, "Faith doesn't pay the bills. Give me something that makes me feel good, draws people, and does good in the community," is the desire of many in the pews. This ideology is the heart of many in churches that are most often associated with biblical Christianity. The world looks on in delight, seeing how far "Christianity" has sunk. Like these folks, Nicodemus is still in the dark and cannot comprehend the Light (John 1:5). Although it is tempting to complain about the modern church and call her back to the pillars of American "Churchianity," what is needed is far more profound.

Paul taught the church in Rome that the gospel is the power of God. He wrote,

The Serpent and the Cross

"For I am not ashamed of the gospel, for it is the power of God for salvation to everyone who believes, to the Jew first and also to the Greek." (Romans 1:16)

Paul lived in the power of God. Although he never got rich from it, the gospel that he preached regenerated the hearts and minds of hundreds who in turn affected thousands. To this day, any truly regenerate person owes their salvation in part to God's work through this man, Paul. His efforts were extraordinary and sacrificial. He would never take any credit for this, but credit and honor are due to him. He was a slave of Christ and as a result of his obedience, we can witness the continual spread of that same gospel throughout the world.

Paul and Jesus preached the same gospel of the Kingdom, and both turned the world upside-down. We Evangelicals also claim to preach the same gospel, but yet our preaching is powerless, our church members are as worldly as the bum on the street, and the world is in love with us. So, what is our problem? Why aren't more churches demonstrably generating the same results as the early churches and Apostles? Why don't we experience the same glory of the redemption of sinners, who in turn testify of His grace until they pass into glory? Why don't we see the same increase in godliness among our members as was among the early disciples of Christ? Why is it that, instead of being sober-minded, dignified, and able teachers of the Word, we see pastors imitating the world by means of skinny jeans, hard rock "worship music," and edgy, satirical sermons? Why is it that so many have resorted to therapeutic preaching so that people can deal with the "issues" in their lives instead of preaching the whole counsel of God (Acts 20:26-27)?[92] In our churches, the man of God has given up his mantle as preacher and embraced his new-found role of counselor.

How can these things be? To be blunt, our gospel is not the gospel of the kingdom. The gospel of the kingdom is just that—it is of the *kingdom.* Jesus told Pilate,

"My kingdom is not of this world. If My kingdom were of this world, then My servants would be fighting so that I would not be handed over to the Jews; but as it is, My kingdom is not of this realm." (John 18:36)

Jesus' kingdom, and the gospel of this kingdom, are not from this earth, nor are they limited to earth's economy. It is a call to the world, the nations, to repent and follow Jesus Christ. It is the task of Christ's disciples to go into the world and make disciples of the people we encounter. The power that accompanies that effort is not that of signs and wonders. It is not personal or church street-appeal, nor monetary investment and large productions. The power that accompanies the gospel of the kingdom is the power inherent in the preached Word of God. That is, it is the ability of God to cause a sinner to hear the Word of God, and lift his head and look toward Jesus Christ. This sinner

---

[92] If you examine this passage which Paul spoke, you will find that those who do not preach accurately the whole counsel of God are guilty of the blood of those in their churches who are stuck in their doctrinal error. We who are leaders in the Church must be careful to protect the sheep, not only from wolves, but *also* from false doctrine.

is caused by God to turn away from the sin that he loves and look toward the very Judge who is hung on the pole for the sins of His people (Matthew 1:21). It is the ability of God to take a sinner and make him or her a saint. It is the ability to enliven a slave of Satan and make him or her a son of God (Matthew 12:25-29). This is power indeed! What other movement in history has such power? There is no other.

Where exactly does the blame lie for the weak gospel found in most churches? The blame is where the blame should be—upon the leaders of the churches. James instructed the men of the churches in Asia Minor not to run too quickly to the office of teacher, because teachers of the Bible are held to a stricter judgment (James 3:1). Why? Because a teacher of God's revelation is directly responsible for communicating the gospel of the kingdom of Jesus Christ. This is a frightening thing to consider, for if a pastor or elder does not work hard to understand the gospel of the kingdom, then he is even more prone to judgment. God will hold that man doubly accountable for his laziness in his study. Paul also taught that an elder in the church must study the word of God in the same way that a specialized workman labors over his own job. He wrote,

Be diligent to present yourself approved to God as a workman who does not need to be ashamed, accurately handling the word of truth. (2 Timothy 2:15)

When a man does not work hard to accurately handle the "word of truth," he should be ashamed of himself. As Paul told Timothy earlier, the man of God needs to be "absorbed in these things" (1 Timothy 4:15). He must abandon all other hopes and dreams for himself and absorb himself in the writings of the Scriptures. When he does this, he will find himself more alert and able to deal with doctrinal confusion.

The gospel that does not include a God who has an eternal plan in Christ Jesus to redeem those whom He, and He alone, chose for Christ is not the gospel of the kingdom. The announcement to the world that the Son has come to His own things should have caused every person alive to tremble and repent at the preaching of Jesus Christ. Instead of repentance, they mocked Him and murdered Him. Not satisfied with His righteousness, they sought to maintain their own by works. Sadly, this same ambition is alive and well in the church today. Far too many want to establish their personal kind of Christianity and not the Christianity of the kingdom.

APPENDIX 1

GOD'S LOVE-WHAT IS IT?

It is not hard to see why we have to answer this question: "What is the love of God?" Although I have endeavored to provide introductory, and summary, information concerning the love of God, I believe it is important to expand upon this in an appendix. The sheer vastness of this topic, God's love, will not allow us to exhaust its meaning, nor will it answer every question raised upon reading. However, we cannot let this issue go without due attention.[93]

Although it is tempting to enter into debates concerning the love of God for the elect or non-elect, I really can't proceed with that until we examine His love as who He is first. That is, we cannot worry about how God's love affects us until we have first examined His love for Himself. Which, to say that God loves Himself ultimately, is a strange thing to assert. If I said that I love myself, you would have nothing to do with me, and rightfully so. However, I am not God. God is not me. To say that God loves Himself is just fine for Himself. There is no contradiction nor is

---

[93] See Ephesians 3:14-21

there anything wrong with it. However, it is a strange thing to hear, unless of course we understand God.

John MacArthur has written,

"In what sense can God call Himself [wayward Israel as seen in Isaiah 63:7-9]'s savior? Here is the sense of it: God revealed Himself as Savior. He manifested His love to the nation. "In all their affliction He was afflicted" (63:9). He poured out His goodness, and lovingkindness and mercy on the nation. And that divine forbearance and longsuffering should have moved them to repentance (Romans 2:4). But instead they responded with unbelief, and their hearts were hardened."[94]

In essence, God's love was demonstrated to Israel and yet Israel did not repent. God's love to them was not met with repentance in a majority of the nation historically. Rather, it was met with a hardened heart and stiffened neck.

This dynamic is the microcosm of how God's love is extended to the world. God's love has been demonstrated to the world by means of the Son of God, His incarnation more specifically. However, the result was that the Son was killed by the world and not received (John 1:10-11). That demonstrates to us the serious state in which the world exists.

In order to establish the kind of love that God has, we must consider the godhead. When we speak of God, we are speaking of the Father, the Son, and the Holy Spirit. It is clear that such a God exists in Scripture. We cannot completely develop

---

[94] John MacArthur, *The Love of God: He Will Do Whatever It Takes to Make Us Holy* (Dallas: Word, 1996), p.115.

that here. However, we can see it clearly in the following passages.

Some of the first indications that God is Three Persons in One God, and thus One God (Deuteronomy 6:4) is in Genesis 1:1-3. There we see that Moses writes that God created the heavens and earth and that the Spirit of God was "oscillating" over the surface of the water. This indicates that the God of v. 1 is distinct from the God of v. 2. This is simply because there was no one else around and the activity of creation is only ascribed to God in Scripture (Revelation 4:11). Thus, the Spirit of God is God. Also, as we continue along in the Bible, we see that the LORD has a Son according to Psalm 2:7. According to Psalm 110:1, David said that the LORD spoke to his Lord, that is Jesus Christ (Hebrew 1:3, 13; 10:13). Further, the writers of the gospels of Matthew, Mark, and Luke indicate to us that at the time of Jesus' baptism the Triunity of God was on full display.[95] It is evident from Scripture that God is comprised of three Persons, distinct in personhood, and yet unified in nature, purpose, and extent.

What is interesting in reference to our study, is that the essential quality of this God is that He loves Himself. Maybe another way to understand that is that God shows love within Himself. Let's look at a few examples.

Jesus said in John 17:24

---

[95] See Matthew 3:16-17; Mark 1:10-11; Luke 3:22.

"Father, I desire that they also, whom You have given Me, be with Me where I am, so that they may see My glory which You have given Me, for You loved Me before the foundation of the world."

Apart from the teaching concerning the apostleship of the men whom Christ chose, notice what the Lord is saying is the basis of His request to have these men with Him where He is-the Father's love for the Son. That is, since the Father loves the Son, the Son's petition would be answered and these men will spend eternity with Him. The Father loved the Son before the foundation of the world. That was the condition and quality of the relationship between the Father and the Son for all of eternity.

Further, the Son loved the Father from all eternity. Jesus said in John 14:31,"...but so that the world may know that I love the Father, I do exactly as the Father commanded Me. Get up, let us go from here." Once again, consider what the Lord is saying here. His demonstration of love for the Father is in view. He wants to show the world that He loves the Father and does that by obeying the Father, even to the point of death. But, again, this is a demonstration of love, love of the Father by the Son. In particular, this is important as it relates to the realities involved in the cross of Jesus Christ. It was on the cross that this righteousness of love was demonstrated. Paul wrote that the righteousness of God was demonstrated publicly on the cross of Jesus Christ (Romans 3:21-26). Foundational to it all was the love of the Son from the Father and the love of the Father from the Son.

Further, we also understand that the Holy Spirit also loves the Father and the Son as evidenced by His obedience to them. The Father will send the Holy Spirit, the same Holy Spirit of Genesis 1:2, to the world (John 14:26) indicating an obedience on the part of the Holy Spirit. This obedience, as indicated by Jesus in John 14:31, is an obedience of love. Love obeys. Further, the Father will send the Holy Spirit at the request of the Son (John 15:26; 16:7). Therefore, the Holy Spirit loves the Father and the Son and obeys them both. This does not demean the Spirit of God. It leaves Him where He is-God. And, as God, He loves God the Father and God the Son.

It is foundational to understand that this love existing between the Father, Son, and Holy Spirit is the highest, purest, and most supreme love. It is a love that is unhindered by sin or anything that defiles. It is a free and eternal love that is willing to obey, even to the point of death. It is the love that God extends to Himself.

Now, having said all of that, we must begin to realize that this love is reserved for God and His people only. This love, which is based upon the nature of God Himself, is not the love that the world enjoys. This love is reserved only for those whom God has created for the Son as much as it is reserved for the Son Himself. Jesus said, "He who has My commandments and keeps them is the one who loves Me; <u>and he who loves Me will be loved</u> <u>by My Father, and I will love him</u> and will disclose Myself to him" (John 14:21, emphasis mine). It is the one who loves Jesus Christ who is loved by the Father. That is, the one who is regenerate is loved by the Father since only the regenerate will love Christ (1 John 4:7-10). When the Lord said this, the disciples realized what He meant. There is a clear distinction in this passage that the love of God is particular to the disciples and distinct from the world. The disciples asked in the following verse, "Lord, what then has happened that you are going to disclose Yourself to us and not to the world?" The disciples are attempting to understand why they would receive the disclosure of the Lord, as well as love of the Lord, and not the world. The disclosure and the love are components of the same work of Jesus Christ. The Lord then said,

"If anyone loves Me, he will keep My word; and My Father *will love him, and We will come to him and make Our abode with* *him. He who does not love Me does not keep My words; and the* *word which you hear is not Mine, but the Father's who sent Me"* *(v.23).*

The fruit of the love for Jesus Christ will be obedience to His Word. The person that asserts that he loves Jesus Christ will demonstrate God's love, which is poured out into his heart (Romans 5:5), by means of keeping of Jesus' teaching, which is really the Father's teaching.[96] The love of Jesus Christ, which is

---

[96] This, of course, is not supporting the idea that we do not have sin in us any longer. We do. Paul indicated that unequivocally in Romans 6-7. It is the basis of our longing for the new creation (Romans 8). However,

the same love of the Father (John 15:9; 17:26), is evident by a person's response to Jesus' Word.

DOES GOD LOVE THE WORLD?

But, for some, the question still remains-"Does God love the world, or not?" The answer is a "yes and no" answer. It depends upon the meaning one ascribes to the word "love."

If "love" is meant as an expression of His nature to the world, regardless of the condition of the world, then yes. However, it must be understood that this is not the quality of love that defines the love between the Father and the Son since this love does not depend upon the righteousness of the recipient. In other words, the world, in all of its darkness, is loved by God because of who God is, not who they are. The love that defines the godhead is predicated upon the absolute purity and holiness of God, which creates unhindered intimacy, and knowledge of one another. This is pure love and is the highest as it refers to the condition of both the Son and the Father.

If "love" is meant is described as unhindered relationship between the world and the Father, no, in that sense, God does

---

the overall direction of a man's life will be a desire to obey as well as some measure of obedience to the Lord Jesus Christ.

not love the world. For example, the world is estranged from God. We know that because the world is hostile toward God, and His Son (John 3:20; cf. Romans 5:10-11). Therefore, by default, the world is not in that unhindered love relationship that exists in the godhead (John 17:25; 15:21). It is made available only to the sons of God (John 14:21; Romans 5:8; cf. Romans 8:38-39; 1 John 3:1).

What needs to be addressed along with this is the issue of whether salvation is actually available to all, or if it is limited to only the elect. For many, the answer to this question decides what one believes about the love of God. That is unfortunate, however, because this topic does not make or break the understanding of God's love. Salvation is only an expression of God's love, a demonstration of it. It is not the express *definition* of it.

As mentioned above, God loves Himself because God is One in Three Persons, the Father, the Son, and the Holy Spirit. They love each other perfectly with unhindered intimacy because absolute righteousness and glory is the basis of the relationship of each Person. This is the condition into which certain men and women will enter one day (John 17:26). This is what John means when he recorded Jesus as saying, "This is eternal life, that they may know You, the only true God, and Jesus Christ, Whom You have sent" (John 17:3). Eternal life is existing in that eternal, unhindered, and permanent, intimacy with the Father, Jesus Christ, and the Holy Spirit (Ephesians 2:17-18). This is eternal life because the only way to get into this relationship is by God's work in putting us there. Only He can remove all transgressions which separate (Psalm 5:4; 92:15). That, in essence, is the reason for the cross. It removes the barriers to this access by means of the death of a Man on behalf of men (Romans 5:6-9). It is in this sense that God was reconciling the world to Himself (Romans 5:18-19). God's work in Jesus Christ is to reconcile His people in the world to Himself. The work of Jesus Christ is the basis for Paul's wording here. He came to seek and save the lost. He came to redeem those who are His. He came to make propitiation for the sins of His people (Hebrews 2:9-17). Yet, these people are located in the world. That is the sense in which God is reconciling the world to Himself. This is, as mentioned in chapter 2, the work of Jesus Christ to the restoration of the kingdom to Himself.

GOD'S LOVE FOR THE KINGDOM

If you have read chapters 6 & 7, you have been introduced to the "eternal purpose of God in Christ Jesus" (Ephesians 3:9-11), and have seen that the kingdom was designed for the sons of God. The sons of the evil one infiltrated it, and we now await the time when the Son of God will remove all stumbling blocks from His kingdom (Matthew 13:41-42). Further, we realize that the sons of God need to be redeemed and that is who we, true Christians, are (Titus 2:11-14). It does not appear that God's intentions are to redeem those who are classified, to borrow from our Lord's teaching from Matthew 25:31-46, as "goats." These goats, or sons of the evil one (Matthew 13:38), can never be redeemed for they are not, from their very existence, sheep. God's sheep, His people, whether Jew or Gentile, are only those who will ever actually enter their kingdom (Matthew 25:34). Thus, goats, or tares, whether Jew or Gentile, will not enter the kingdom but will suffer the eternal lake of fire. This is God's eternal purpose in Christ Jesus. Unless one understands, and believes, in the absolute holiness of God, the realities described above will be questioned. By that I mean, some might impugn God for casting so many into the Lake of Fire instead of simply saving them from it, as He will do to the sheep. However, Paul wrote, "What shall we say then? There is no injustice with God, is there? May it never be?" (Romans 9:14). We might philosophically disagree with this because we would have to believe that God would rescue as many as He can. We might consider that love. However, the reality is, that is not love. At least, not the love that loves God first. In reality, if we love God, we would have to be zealous for His own glory before we ever desire the benefit of man. Yet, this does not indicate that God enjoys the death of the wicked. He does not. As mentioned before, it is a grievous thing to Him.

The death of the wicked, even in the zealous love that God has for Himself, is not pleasing to Him. Ezekiel is often referred to along these lines. The prophet wrote, "For I have no pleasure in the death of anyone who dies," declares the Lord God. "Therefore, repent and live" (Ezekiel 18:32). However, we must realize that God did not say this in a vacuum. The context demonstrates the justice of God in that the sinner who repents will live and the sinner who does not will die (v. 23). The sinner who produces repentance in himself (v. 32) will then be forgiven of his sins and restored to God and covenant blessing (Leviticus 26:40ff.).[97] But, that is the issue, isn't it. A sinner cannot produce repentance in his heart (Jeremiah 13:23). The sinner who sins will die (v. 4). Thus, the sense in this is that of imploring Israel to repent, otherwise He will punish the sinner by death (v. 18). It is true about God, obviously, that He does not desire the death of anyone. However, His righteousness is unbending and demands conformity.

If you consider all the deaths that have occurred in human history, including the flood as well as natural disasters, wars, and pestilence, you will quickly realize how much heartbreak God must have at the death of the billions of wicked men and women. But please, as much as that pulls on our heart-strings, realize that God's righteousness is never at stake because of their deaths. He is the executioner of all who sin (Genesis 2:16-17). As much as it grieves His heart, and it does, I am sure, immeasurably (Genesis 6:5-7), it is still right for YHWH to punish sins by death.

---

[97] This was God's demand as told in the Law (Deuteronomy 10:16; cf. Jeremiah 4:4).

Appendix 2

THE FAILURE OF COVENANT THEOLOGY TO UNDERSTAND THE GOSPEL

This appendix will not be important for many because they are simply not aware of the issues involved in what is written here. However, for some, especially as it relates to the gospel, what is written here is extremely important. That is because the motivations and purposes behind God's saving work are crucial to understand. The gospel is the product of that purpose. If we do not understand the purposes of God, the details of such a purpose, and the origin of that purpose, we cannot fully grasp the content and meaning in the gospel of Jesus Christ.

Covenant Theology (CT) is a system of theology that purports two (or three) "covenants" in eternity past and at creation, that lay the groundwork for the saving work of God. The primary covenant purported is the Covenant of Works, as the system calls it. This covenant is described as the agreement between God and Adam, in the garden, wherein both God and Adam were the contractual parties. The esteemed Westminster Confession states, "The first covenant made with man was a covenant of works, wherein life was promised to Adam; and in him to his prosperity, upon condition of perfect and personal obedience."[98] Herman Witsius, in his foundational work for Covenantalists entitled, *The Economy of the Covenants Between God and Man* (Thomas Nelson: London, 1822), devotes a large section to the "contracting parties" of the Covenant of Works. It is said there that God, upon creating man, enacted a covenant with him that Adam should fulfill upon the penalty of death if he does not fulfill it. Adam consented; thus, the covenant of works. The assertion is that God "cut" a covenant (Hebrew, berit) , which was binding for Adam and for all man, at that time of creation, which in turn would demonstrate loyalty on Adam's part. In this particular section of Dr. Witsius' book are a number of Scripture references and quotes. However, by and large, they are misdirected and misleading. The truth of the references are unquestionable. The application of those truths to an assumed system, as found in the Covenant of Works, is unbiblical.

For example, on pages 46-47, the author states that God is one Party to the covenant, man the other. Thus when

"[Adam] consents thereto, embracing the good promised by God, engaging to an exact observance of the condition required; and upon the violation thereof, voluntarily owning himself obnoxious to the threatened curse. This the scripture calls... "to

---

[98] *Westminster Confession of Faith*, 1646, chapter VII, section II.

enter into covenant with the Lord," Deut. xxix.12. "and to enter into

a curse and an oath," Neh. 29.""[99]

What Dr. Witsius is saying is that when God created Adam, He and Adam made an agreement by virtue of his being created, bearing His image. Thus, once Adam realized the stipulations of this creation agreement, he agreed to the contract. He entered into a covenant with the Lord, in the same way that is spoken of in Deuteronomy 29:12 in regards to Israel. Thus, the author puts the same binding agreement that Israel experienced with God through the Law of Moses upon Adam saying that they were equal. Another way to say it is that Dr. Witsius takes a postulated covenant and equates it with the reality of a clearly written covenant and makes them equal. Well, not really. In reality, Adam's so-called covenant supersedes Israel's covenant.

Did God make a covenant with Adam in the same way that He made a covenant with Israel? Further, does it matter? Let's look at this carefully.

First, there is never mentioned in Scripture that God made a binding, legal, agreement with Adam. In all of Paul's writings (as well as the prophets) about Adam, he does not once state that Adam reneged on his contractual agreement

---

[99] *The Economy of the Covenants,* pp. 46-47.

with God. There might be two objections at this point. One: "What about Hosea 6:7? It clearly says that Adam broke his covenant." Does it? What does Hosea actually say? Adam is not the subject of the sentence. Israel is the subject, as evidenced by the personal pronoun, 'they'. They transgressed the covenant. What covenant? The only covenant Scripture indicates that God made with Israel and they continually broke (see the context of the entire book of Hosea, for example). However, does it say that Adam broke a covenant also? No. It says that Adam transgressed (cf. Romans 5:18). It does not say that he transgressed a covenant since there is no recorded covenant in Genesis 1-2. The phrase, "like Adam", is a comparison to the transgression and not the covenant. Besides, the better translation would say, "Like a man" and not "like Adam" since the article does not precede the word 'adam', which, when taken with the article, refers to the individual Adam. However, when the article is not there, it is man in general since the word 'adam' means 'man'. This is the only verse in all of Scripture that actually uses 'Adam' and 'covenant' in proximity to each other and we can see that this is not even referring to a broken covenant made with Adam.

Some might say, "But the evidence of a covenant is there; stipulations, warnings, and punishment for failure." Really? Did God need a covenant in order to maintain order in the garden? Did Adam have to agree to the terms of a covenant in order to go about his day? The observation of death upon disobedience, does that demand a covenant structure? According to the Apostle Paul, no.

> *Therefore, just as through one man sin entered into the world, and death through sin, and so death spread to all men, because all sinned—*

> *for until the Law sin was in the world, but sin is not imputed when there is no law.*

> *Nevertheless death reigned from Adam until Moses, even over those who had not sinned in the likeness of the offense of Adam, who is a type of Him who was to come. (Romans 5:12-14)*

It is clear that Adam did fall, and miserably so. He did sin. He did transgress God's command. But this does not demand a covenant structure. Paul writes that through one man, sin entered the world and with it came death. We understand this event as that time when Adam, against the command of God, ate from the Tree of the Knowledge of Good and Eevil (Genesis 3:1-7;cf. Genesis 2:16-17). However, Paul does not equate the disobedience of Adam to the breaking of a legal contract, i.e. a covenant. Death spread to all men because all sinned. This is because until the Law (Mosaic) sin was in the world, but it was not imputed to man (Romans 5:12-13). What does that mean? From Adam to Moses, the punishment of Adam was experienced-death. However, that same offense of

Adam is not experienced by every man. Mankind, as coming from Adam, died because they were "in Adam." However, they did not sin that sin which Adam did, namely eating of the Tree of the Knowledge of Good and Evil. They were made sinners as coming from Adam, but they, themselves, did not each take of the tree and eat. Therefore, sin, or the transgression of a commandment, was not legally marked down on their account as a broken law, i.e. imputed. Paul is right, sin is not imputed when there is no law. After Adam, no one else ate of the Tree of the Knowledge of Good and Evil. So, technically, they did not sin. However, mankind is alienated from God and dead in their sinful natures. But, it was not until the Law of Moses that sin could be legally imputed to each man and thus each man bear the weight of his own transgression. Paul is saying that Adam did not break a covenant. Adam disobeyed God. Big difference. The stipulations of a so-called covenant were not broken because there was no covenant. We know this because Paul says that sin was not imputed. That is, Adam did not break a legal agreement. He did disobey. He did transgress. But the legal aspect, which CT asserts to be present, was not there. Thus, there was no covenant. It is simply God's creation rising up in rebellion against his Maker.

For some readers, this is pure semantics. However, how closely you define these things determines which direction you go in other doctrines. For the Covenantalist, since they assume a covenant here, they are free to assume other covenants, namely the Covenant of Grace. Thus, from there, they feel the freedom to assume other things as well. For example, they might feel the need to assume that since we are all under a covenant of grace, then Israel has merged with the church and there are no national promises made to Israel since they don't exist anymore in God's plan. Or, they might assume that they can take a text of Scripture and install a second meaning into that passage (a Covenantalist handles most of the Old Testament this way). To some, these issues are inconsequential. However, to God, they are not. The assertion that God made a covenant with Adam, which he broke, misrepresents what actually happened, and thus distorts God's revelation of Scripture, thus robbing God of glory. This is no small assertion.

So, what actually happened? Just what Paul said happened. Adam disobeyed a command of God. A command which, if obeyed, would maintain (not create) fellowship with God forever. As one unnamed writer stated (as quoted from within Dr. Witsius' work and he summarily disagrees with)

"Prior to the fall there was properly no law. There… a state of friendship and love obtained, such as is the natural state of a son with respect to a parent, and which is what nature affects. But when that love is violated, then a precept comes to be superadded: and that love, which before was voluntary, (as best agreeing with its nature; for that can scarcely be called love, unless voluntary) falls under a precept, and passes into a law, to be enforced then with commination and coercion; which rigour of coercion properly constitutes a law." (Economy, p.61).

He is right. Paul wrote in Galatians 5:22-23,

But the fruit of the Spirit is love, joy, peace, patience, kindness, goodness, faithfulness, gentleness, self-control; against such things there is no law.

There is no law to regulate love. You do not need regulation of divine love and relationship, such as that for which Adam was created. Adam was created in a condition of righteousness such that he was able to fellowship with God. This relationship is as a son to a father (Luke 3:38), not a servant to a master. A slave/master relationship exists with Satan and his subjects (John 8:31-44). Our relationship to God can also be described as slave and Master (Ephesians 6:6). Yet, ultimately, we are sons (Revelation 21:7) and as a true son, we will serve our Father just like Jesus Christ does as well as reign with Him (Revelation 22:3,5). Still, Adam was created as a son, in the likeness of the Son. There is no law, or covenant, to regulate that condition. It was not until the fall that that relationship was severed, Adam apostatized, Satan became lord over him, and began to rule. Thus, when the Son makes you free, you shall be free indeed-free to be a son again (John 1:12-

13; 8:31; Galatians 3:26). Therefore, when you say that there was a covenant between God and Adam, you are then distorting the love of God, and His image, and making it something other than it is.

Covenant Theology asserts that God made a covenant with Adam in which if Adam were obedient, he would inherit eternal life. If he were disobedient, he would die. Or to put another way, if he obeyed, he would be blessed. If he disobeyed, he would be cursed. The backdrop for this reasoning is the assertion that the components of covenants are present in the narrative of Genesis 1-2. "The substance of covenant is the stuff that forms the contents of Genesis 1-3".[100] These components also are present in the Ancient Near Eastern (ANE) treaties identified in archaeological finds over the years. In comparing those finds, including significant discoveries like the treaties of the Hittites and the Ebla Tablets, with the biblical texts, it is believed that God followed the same pattern as those treaties and covenants as written in the ANE discoveries in the creation of the world.

I would like to challenge that assumption and clarify a few things concerning this hypothesis. Specifically, I do not believe that Moses is writing as one would from the structure of ANE treaties. Further, the components of a covenant are not present in the text of Genesis 1-2.

---

[100] Meredith Kline, "Two Adams, Two Covenants of Work; Selected Readings From *Kingdom Prologue*", published online by www.upper-register.com, 2007, p.1 site accessed 1/4/2014.

First, it is important that we insert a foundational tenant of Scripture, namely the doctrine of inerrancy. Inerrancy states that the Scriptures, in the autographs, are inspired by God through the instrument of human authors and as such the resultant text is infallible, true, and authoritative. Also, the basis of the inerrancy of Scripture, and the veracity of the resultant copies of those inerrant letters/books, is that God, who cannot lie (Titus 1:2), is the source of the information contained therein. That is, although man may have used sources other than dictation from God (e.g. Luke 1:1-4), the resulting text of Scripture is nonetheless truth and has God as the source of that information. Inerrancy is also claimed by CT as well. Why is inerrancy significant to our discussion? Because, when speaking of covenantal language in Genesis 1-2, A) does history interpret the event of creation, or B) does creation define and interpret history? The only correct answer is B, Scripture, and its account of creation, defines and interprets history. Therefore, let us consider the assertion that all the components of ANE treaties are present in the creation narrative of Genesis 1-2 as patently false. There are a number of reasons, which I will give below, but begin by considering that God did not follow the conventions of culture (of ANE or otherwise) when He established the foundations of the earth. If it is asserted that God's work in creation followed the pattern of ANE treaties/covenants, then we have committed eisegesis saying that God's creation work was patterned after ANE cultural norms. Surely, inerrancy cannot be maintained with that assertion since creation came before the Hittites.

Second, the components of a covenant/treaty are not present in Genesis 1-2. The general components of the Covenant of Works are usually listed as preamble/prologue, contractual parties, stipulations, blessings for obedience, curses for disobedience, and concluding remarks usually calling upon witnesses to the agreement. Michael Horton, author and host of White Horse Inn, a Christian radio show from a Reformed perspective, also describes a "typical" covenant arrangement and attributes that back into Genesis:

" In addition, the literary elements of covenant-making seem to be present in the Genesis narrative, especially as interpreted by the rest of Scripture. Even in Genesis 1-3 we recognize the features of a covenant that we have delineated: a historical prologue setting the stage (Genesis 1-2), stipulations (2:16-17), and sanctions (2:17b) over which Eve and the serpent argue (3:1-5) and which are finally carried out in the form of judgment (3:8-19).101

Kim Riddlebarger, professor at Westminster Seminary of Escondido, California and pastor of Christ Reformed Church, Anaheim, CA., lists them in summary form as:

"Although the term "covenant of works" does not appear in the creation account, all of the elements of such a

---

101 Michael Horton, *The God of Promise,* (Grand Rapids: Baker Books, 2006), p. 90.

covenant are clearly present in Eden. First, there are two parties involved (Adam and his creator), with God sovereignly imposing the terms of this covenant upon Adam and his descendants. Second, there is a condition set forth by God as spelled out in Genesis 2:17–"but of the tree of the knowledge of good and evil you shall not eat, for in the day that you eat of it you shall surely die." Although this condition comes in the form of a specific prohibition (if you eat from the tree you will die), it can also be framed as a positive theological principle which describes the very essence of this covenant: "Do this [i.e., obey by not eating] and live." Third, there is a blessing promised upon perfect obedience (eternal life) as well as a threatened curse (death) for any act of disobedience. If Adam obeys his creator and does not eat from the tree, then he will receive God's promised blessing–eternal life. But should Adam eat from the tree, then he will come under the covenant curse– which is death."102

If we simply use these writings as our starting points, we will discover that the ideal of the Covenant of Works is, in fact, the philosophy of man and not a true explanation of what God actually did.

First, Michael Horton indicates that the entire narrative of Genesis 1-3 fits into the ANE structure. Unfortunately, he

---

102 Westminster Seminary California, blog, http://wscal.edu/blog/entry/3608, accessed 9/4/2012.

does not seem to comprehend that the creation of the world and the cosmos does not fit into covenantal/treaty structure. Although Moses wrote during the time when the Near East was not ancient, creation occurred before ANE culture. When these things are read into the biblical text, the text is treated as some literary piece and not actual history. Such is the common failure of CT.

Second, Dr. Riddlebarger, who has done much to confuse the Scriptures, states that if Adam would obey God, he would receive access to the Tree of Life. Once eating the fruit, he would then live forever. It is further stated that Adam is on a kind of probation to prove his obedience. There are a few problems with that teaching, however. Most CT teachers repeat Genesis 2:17, "…but from the tree of the knowledge of good and evil you shall not eat, for in the day that you eat from it you will surely die." Along with this verse is the usual statement that this indicates a kind of test for Adam. In fact, this "condition" becomes the hinge-pin for much in CT. Adam failed to maintain the condition by breaking the covenant, and thus he died as per this verse. The converse, they reason, is also true. If Adam does obey, then he will receive blessing. One glaring problem is the fact that the biblical text says in the previous verse, "The Lord God commanded the man, saying, "From any tree of the garden you may eat freely…" (v.16). Adam already had access, free access, to any other tree in the garden, including the Tree of Life. In fact, both eating of every other tree in the garden and not eating of the tree of the knowledge of good and evil are all under the umbrella of a "command" (v.16). It is just as much a command to eat freely as it is to not eat. This is also verified by the fact that the Tree of Life needed to be guarded from Adam and Eve after the fall (Genesis 3:24). He did, in fact, have access to that tree even after his disobedience! The reasoning with CT is that if Adam exhibits perfect obedience to the command (the stipulations of the "covenant"), then by not eating of the tree of the knowledge of good and evil he will then, in time, be able to have access to the tree of life, by the sheer fact that he will still be alive to do so. This conditional existence of Adam, according to CT, is the basis for the rest of their assumptions in theology. However, there were no conditions in the garden, and thus there was nothing for Adam to agree to. This is not a contractual agreement between two parties. In fact, is was not a "royal grant" either since God does not promise to benefit Adam in the least. Adam was already blessed, already possessed life, and already walked with God:

Let me reiterate. Adam already had free and unhindered access to the tree of life (Genesis 2:16). There was no condition, whatsoever, for Adam to be able to go up to that tree and take of its fruit and eat. He was already given free access by the Creator.

This is crucial to realize. Since there was no contractual condition for which Adam must attain, then there was no covenant. Since there was no covenant, this arrangement in the garden does not follow ANE treaty structure, or anything of the sort. God's work in creation is simply an expression of His will. To assert and teach that Adam's eating of the tree of life is based upon not eating of the tree of the knowledge of good and evil is to 1) miss the actual words of the text, 2) misrepresent what God has done in creation, and 3) diverge from sound biblical revelation on the matter, and thus maintain an apostate position, thereby harming the church for whom the truth of Scripture belongs (1 Timothy 3:15).

Third, CT also asserts that God would bless Adam if he obeyed, and curse Adam if he did not. That is not true. As already stated, God already blessed Adam (Genesis 1:28). He already had life (Genesis 2:7). In fact, the restriction to the tree of life post-fall indicates that he would have been confirmed in some kind of perpetual physical life that could be sustained forever. That is not to say, however, that he would have inherited "eternal life" such as we have in Christ (i.e. partaking of the divine nature – 1 Peter 1:3). We know this because God indicates that if Adam and Eve, in their punished, fallen state, would have eaten of that tree, they would have been confirmed in that state. The tree itself, having properties that sustained and strengthened (see Revelation 22:2; cf. Ezekiel 47:12), did not possess the quality of eternal, divine, life since Adam and

Eve would have been sustained in their fallen condition if they would have eaten of that tree. Therefore, to say that if they would have obeyed, they would have satisfied the covenantal agreement with God and would have been given access to the tree of life so that they would live eternally is false. Adam already had access to the tree of life (Genesis 2:16). Adam and Eve were already blessed of God (Genesis 1:28a). The tree of life simply perpetuated physical life forever, which is not the same thing as the quality of divine life that CT attributes to it.

In none of these arrangements do we see conditions placed upon the man. God did not say, "Adam, if you obey Me, I will give you to eat of the tree of life." He already had access to that tree under no grants or conditions. God simply created the tree for Adam and his offspring. Nor did He say to Adam, "If you obey Me, I will bless you." God had already established a blessed state for Adam and his wife. There were no conditions, and thus no covenant. The text of inspired Scripture indicates that God blessed them (Genesis 1:28) and that was not contingent upon obedience. They already had it! It was the will of God. Once again, since nowhere in the text is there indication of conditions for blessing or access to the tree of life, then there is no covenant. Covenants are based upon conditions. Even unilateral covenants, such as with Abraham (Genesis 12:1-3; 17:4-6), require a certain attainment of righteousness.

However, all we have in the actual text of Scripture in Genesis 1-2 is God creating and giving freely to the man, the woman, and their children of His provision without cost or covenant. To say that the command not to eat from the tree presupposes a covenant is reading into the text to a detrimental degree. If anything, the command of God not to eat from the tree of the knowledge of good and evil was a demonstration of the desire for Christ-like obedience from Adam since he was made in the image of God. How? Because the obedience would have been generated from love and subjection to the Father in the same way that the Son loves and subjects Himself to the Father (John 15:10; 1 Corinthians 11:3). Again, love does not need a law (Galatians 5:22-23). This is why Luke describes Adam as a "son of God" (Luke 3:38).

Since the influence of CT is widespread, especially throughout the Young, Restless, and Reformed people, there needs to be accountability for the mishandling of Scripture in such a fashion as is demonstrated by Covenant Theology. From beginning to end, it is not based upon proper exegesis of the actual text of Scripture, but rather the philosophical musings of men throughout the centuries which have dealt a harmful blow, overall, to the Scripture. Although the gospel itself was recovered by the Reformers, the need to continue a reformation stands. There needs to be a recovery of the authority of the Scripture once again. This authority is only understood and perceived through a hermeneutic of the grammar of a text and the historical context in which the text exists. Once the foundation of CT is laid down as truth, the Scripture cannot hardly be recognized since, by and large, its veracity and literality is compromised many times over, especially in such areas as creation, and eschatology. Both the beginning and the ending of God's Word suffer a harmful blow by the likes of CT to the degree that we do not understand from whence we came, nor for what we have to look forward. Let us truly "keep reforming" and return to a proper, text-centered, study of God's holy, inerrant, and precious, Word.

What motivated God to initiate His saving work? The Covenantalist avers that it was an

"…inter-Trinitarian pact made in eternity past, in which the Father designed, the Son agreed to undertake, and the Spirit agreed to apply the results of redemption." 103 According to CT, God the Father and God the Son undertook a "pact", or covenant, that Christ would satisfy the Father and do so on behalf of the elect. This is the foundation, they say, of all the other covenants. However, unlike the other covenants of CT, this particular covenant does not get as much press.

According to Dr. Witsius again, the initial passage that speaks of this Covenant of Redemption (CR) is Luke 22:29,

---

103

(http://www.monergism.com/thethreshold/articles/onsite/qna/work sgraceredmpt.html, accessed 10/2/2012).

which reads, "…and just as My Father has granted Me a kingdom, I grant you." 104 If I were to presuppose a conclusion, like CT does here, I can easily concede that this would speak of a kingdom which was "covenanted" to Jesus before time. However, right hermeneutics would ask, "What does the context say?" Thus, in the next verse we read, "…that you may eat and drink at My table in My kingdom, and you will sit on thrones judging the twelve tribes of Israel." Just as is taught by our Lord in and Matthew 19:28 and elsewhere, this is not a kingdom promise because of a covenant between the Father and the Son in eternity past. This kingdom is reserved for the covenant fulfillment of David's promise of 2 Samuel 7:13, 16 (cf. Psalm 89; see also Daniel 7:22; Revelation 20:4). The teaching of the inherited kingdom of Jesus Christ is a vast, and easily verifiable, teaching of Scripture. Nowhere in that amount of data is an 'inter-Trinitarian pact' spoken of or alluded to. It is easily, and consistently, refuted by reason of the actual covenants historically promised by God. The entire paradigm of the true, biblical, covenants, then, is undermined by the illusory covenants of CT. This is a very grave error.

A further error that I see repeated by CT is taking actual terms, events, and truths and superimposing the "covenantal" structure over them such that they become actually subject to the philosophy of CT. As R. Scott Clark has written,

---

104 Witsius, *The Economy Of The Covenants* p. 166.

"Covenant theology structures all of Biblical revelation.[105] Is this true? Does CT actually structure all biblical revelation? No, this is not true, since the Bible does not actually teach CT. However, what is happening is that CT is 'extrabiblical' and this extrabiblical system is being imposed upon inerrant Scripture. The Covenant of Redemption is a very good case in point.

Michael Horton has written, "The covenant of redemption, therefore, is as clearly revealed in Scripture as the Trinity and the eternal decree to elect, redeem, call, justify, sanctify, and glorify a people for the Son".[106] But, taking apples and pasting them to an orange tree does not make the orange tree an apple tree.

You can't take the fruit of God's true work in time, and affix it to a man-made system and redefine what God has actually done. In an effort to support his claim, Dr. Horton refers to those wonderful passages in the gospel of John wherein Jesus teaches that the Father has given some (people) to the Son (see John 6:39, 10:29; 17:2, 4-10 etc.). However, just to get straight to the point, if we will once again notice the context of John 6:37-30, for example, we will see repeatedly that this "giving" is the result of the sovereign will of the

---

[105] R. Scott Clark, "Theses on Covenant Theology", http://clark.wscal.edu/covtheses.php, accessed 10/2/2012.

[106] (Horton, *God of Promise* , p.82)

Father (e.g. John 6:37, 38, 39, 40). So, in that scenario, how is it that there was an agreement between the Son and the Father, to say nothing of the Father and the elect? Otherwise, the Father's will would not be free to do all that He would, and thus be sovereign. The Father's will would be bound to an agreement, or some other motivation, that would actually add to His will. That would not, then, allow for absolute sovereign freedom to do all according to the kind intention of His will (Ephesians 1:5). Herein is the irony: Covenantalists make ideal Arminians.

Instead of asserting and maintaining the biblical understanding of God's sovereignty, they insist that God's free will was actually bound by an agreement made between the Father and the Son prior to creation. Thus, the elect, too, can agree to the terms of this agreement, and/or other agreements, and enter into the redemption that is insisted upon because of this so-called Covenant of Redemption. In other words, man, once again, has a say in his salvation. This impugns the sovereignty of God, which those holding to CT so strongly, arrogantly, insist they believe. Yet, when compared with Scripture, we see the arrogance of man contributing to the pure, undefiled, will of God to sovereignly elect whom He will according to His kind intention.

What does the Bible actually say about all this?

The Father commanded the Son to ask the nations and the earth of Him (Psalm 2:8). God created the world for the Son for that purpose-that the Son would inherit the nations, comprised of people, and the earth, the soil upon which we stand. However, due to Satan's deceptive interaction, he planted the seeds of the sons of the evil one (Matthew 13:38), believing that his diabolical work would threaten the sons of the kingdom, causing them to remain sinful and thus be lost to judgment. However, the heart of God's plan is to rescue, or "save," those whom God has designed to give to the Son. The Son to enter into human history and become a Man; Man who was made in His own image and likeness, and die the death that man so-rightly deserved. The Spirit of God empowered Christ by giving Him signs and wonders such that He would fulfill Scripture, which said the Messiah would perform such signs verifying Who He was. The Son would be punished by the Father, die, then rise again. He would then ascend to share the throne of His Father until He re-enters earth and assumes a throne promised to the Seed of David, Himself the Seed of Abraham, thus the Seed of the woman. He would rule, fulfilling the promises upon which the true, biblical, covenants were made in history, for a time, as promised to Israel. Then, to restore the sovereign rule of the Father over everything, He, the Son, will return all things to the Father, and subject Himself to

Him as well. Is all of this to happen because of a covenant? No. This is all

"...according to His purpose who works all things after the counsel of His will...to the praise of His glory." Ephesians 1:11b, 12b

Does His glory involve a pre-temporal covenant? No. It is the simple exertion of sovereign will. It is simply the will of the Father commanding the subjected (but not inferior) Son who obeys because He loves His Father, and for no other motivation (John 14:31). Thus, sending the Spirit to, in fact, create new creations from dead and sinful ones. The Son will subject all things to the Father once again, after He has vanquished all His enemies, so that the Father's supremacy will be restored over all creation and the Father may be all in all (1 Corinthians 15:28), just like it was before Genesis 1:1. To add to that scenario is to add to actual revelation. It is to add to God's purposes. It is to add to God and Who He actually is and what He has actually done. CT does this. Covenantal Theology needs to be held accountable for the confusion it has caused.

APPENDIX 3

THE ROLE OF THE NATIONS IN THE GOSPEL OF THE KINGDOM

The understanding of the nations of the world in the Scriptures is a vast, and often overlooked, subject. Yet, as we will see, it is one that is essential to the gospel and the kingdom. What do we understand by the term "nations"? For some, they consider the nation in which they currently exist. For others, they consider the nation on the other side of the globe that is going to war. For others, the consideration turns to history, or the forming of a nation, such as The United States of America.

However, when the Bible considers the nations, it does not necessarily refer to nations in these ways. In the end, the Bible will not care whether a nation was at war, newly created, or successful on its fiscal policies. God will not be impressed with any of the above in that day that Jesus Christ judges the nations. What is the basis of judgment, and thus the most essential import of the nations? Jesus Christ will judge according to who is a sheep and who is a goat. According to Matthew 25:31-46 (esp. vv. 32-33), the most essential character of those that comprise a nation is whether or not they are sheep or goats. The evidence of such condition is the acceptance, or rejection, of Jesus Christ. Since the judgment of the nations is dependent upon this position, then it is incumbent upon us, the church, to announce this to the nations. That is exactly why Matthew recorded Jesus' final instructions in Matthew 28:18-20 saying

> And Jesus came up and spoke to them, saying, "All authority has been given to Me in heaven and on earth.
>
> "Go therefore and make disciples of all the nations, baptizing them in the name of the Father and the Son and the Holy Spirit,
>
> teaching them to observe all that I commanded you; and lo, I am with you always, even to the end of the age."

If one would take hold of a concordance and look up the word "nations" and begin working through the Scripture every time this word is used, he would find that the concept of a "nation" is prominent in the record of Scripture.[107] As we attempt to build a "Theology of the Nations" in this appendix, we will quickly realize the significance of the nations in God's eternal plan.

---

[107] Using Logos Bible Software (www.logos.com), there were 483 hits on the term "nations" when I made a search through the entire Bible. That may not seem like much considering the thousands of words that are in the Bible. However, the significance lies in what the key passages of the Bible do say about the nations.

WHERE DID THE NATIONS OF THE WORLD COME FROM?

The origin of the nations is explicitly taught in the Bible, thankfully. The origins of the nations of the world, and what determined their nationality are recorded for us in the tenth and eleventh chapters of the book of Genesis. In that inerrant, inspired record, we will find that the nations came into existence by means of a judgment. Yet, the judgment was not the separating of the peoples into nations. The judgment was the response of God to the people because of a *refusal* to separate into nations.

The word translated into the English word "nations" is the Hebrew term גּוֹיִם, (pronounced *'goy-eem'*). The word originated from the idea of a confluence of waters from different streams flowing into one large stream.[108] The idea is a confluence of multiple separate "streams" of people from different regions, languages, and families. As the nations existed in the historical record, they are basically all separated, as will be explained below, into separate groups of people with distinctions unique to them such that they would be identified as a nation. The creation of God was to have all the peoples spread out upon the earth with one region (the entire planet itself) and one language (see

---

[108] גּוֹי, see also גֵּוָה II. Wilhelm Gesenius and Samuel Prideaux Tregelles. *Gesenius' Hebrew and Chaldee Lexicon to the Old Testament Scriptures.* (Grand Rapids: Eerdmans, 1957), p.162-163.

Genesis 11:1). However, the purpose of God established the separation of the peoples from one family, in one region, with one language, to multiple families, in multiple regions, with multiple languages.

Genesis 10:32 indicates that all the nations of the earth originate from three men: Shem, Ham, and Japheth. These men were the sons of Noah and, along with their wives, accompanied Noah on the Ark in order to escape the flood judgment. After the Ark landed, and the world-wide flood waters subsided into the oceans (Genesis 8:1-3) and all the inhabitants of the Ark exited the Ark to enter the new world which was devastated by the judgment. No one survived the flood except those upon the Ark. There was no one else but eight people on the entire planet.

This is why the Scripture records that all the nations originated from Shem, Ham, and Japheth, the sons of Noah. As men began, once again, to populate the earth (Genesis 9:19), the condition of their hearts stayed the same (Genesis 8:21). Just as it did prior to the flood, the condition of the world grew worse until God judged the world again. However, He committed Himself to never send a deluge upon the earth again (Genesis 9:11-16). However, He cannot tolerate the wickedness in His kingdom forever (Genesis 6:3). The next judgment was significant and effective. However, it did not include the annihilation of all the inhabitants of the earth.

THE CREATION OF THE NATIONS

Chapter 10 of Genesis begins with this statement: "Now these are *the records of* the generations of Shem, Ham, and Japheth, the sons of Noah; and sons were born to them after the flood." This is one of six times that the word "generations" is used in the book of Genesis. It is usually acknowledged that these uses were put into place by Moses in order to "frame-up" the book of Genesis around key historical figures.[109] It is also used in Genesis 2:4 to end the narrative of the creation of the cosmos from Genesis 1:1-2:3. The idea is to catalogue significant events in the history of the subject of the generations, whether a man or creation itself. Genesis 10:1 begins the generations of the sons of Shem, Ham, and Japheth, the sons of Noah. The listings in that chapter are those which occurred after a "separation" which itself occurred after the flood (Genesis 10:32). Genesis 11:1-9 gives the history of that separation which occurred after the flood. That separation occurred as a result of the act of God upon the inhabitants of the earth for their efforts in building the city of Babel (Genesis 11:8-9). In that city, the people of the land were constructing a massive tower that they were confident would reach into heaven. It was obvious that they were attempting, as Psalm 2:1-3 indicates, to rage against the Lord and break off His

---

[109] The Hebrew translated "generations" is תּוֹלְדֹת. It has multiple uses in the biblical record (See Genesis 5:1; 6:9; 10:1; 11:10, 27; 25:19). Used here in Genesis it refers, usually, to the record of the time spent by a significant individual in relation to the descendants of the Seed line of the Messiah (see Genesis 3:15; cp. Genesis 5; 1 Chronicles 1:1-2:8).

fetters from themselves. They were avoiding the express command of YHWH to spread out over the earth and rule (Genesis 1:28). In their rebellion, they refused to do so. So, God did it for them. The act of spreading out over the earth was not the judgment upon the people. The changing of vocabulary and dialect was.

Therefore, we have in this act of God what Paul described in Acts 17:26, "...and He made from one man every nation of mankind to live on all the face of the earth, having determined their appointed times and the boundaries of their habitation." It was God who caused the nations to be formed. The nations existed immediately, as opposed to being established over time as might have happened had Adam and Eve never disobeyed God, by the ability of God to pick up entire groups of people and relocate them into a region of His choice and that they might maintain that distinction by means of their language.

There are three aspects to the determination of the nation: family, language, and land. This identified a nation, as far as is recorded by Moses. God separated the earth by means of His power to do so. In doing that, He did not split apart the family, but rather kept them intact. He gave large numbers of families a unique language, and then took those families and placed them into a geographic location of His choosing (see Genesis 10:5; 20; 31-32).[110] Once there, they were a nation. This is the biblical, and only accurate, record of the origin of the nations. It is from these

---

[110] It is significant that the prophets tell us that Jesus will bring all the nations back together again and separate them into one of two categories, sheep or goat (Isaiah 66:18; Joel 3:1-17; Matthew 25:31-33).

nations, primarily, that the other lesser nations arose. The nations as they exist today are simply splinters from those original nations that God created upon His earth.

WHERE ARE THE NATIONS GOING?

In understanding the origin of the nations, we can then move on and appreciate the role of the nations in the history of the world, as well as their future. This is not so much from a secularly anthropological point of view as it is from a biblical point of view. Psalm 2:7-9 sums up the role of the nations, both their origin and their fulfillment. The decree mentioned there is one from the Father to the Son in eternity past. In that discussion, the Father commanded the Son to ask of Him the nations and the earth. Neither nations nor the earth existed then. However, it reveals to us the plan of God and gives rise to the explanation of all creation-it was created by the Father, through the Son, for the Son (Romans 11:36; 1 Corinthians 8:6; Colossians 1:16). God's glorious original design created in Genesis 1-2 was that mankind would be fruitful, multiply, and fill the earth while subduing it in order to rule it (Genesis 1:28). In doing that, the existence at that time would be separated, naturally, into regions and thus nations, yet without language distinctions.

We know that this is God's original design because it becomes His ultimate design as well. As we jump from creation to consummation, we see that the condition of the cosmos, including the earth, ends the very same way it begins, and yet with improvements (to say the least!). This subject is far too vast to research fully in an appendix. However, we can get the idea of the existence of the nations from a few passages that guide our thinking.

The typical Christian believes that their *eternal* dwelling place after they die is heaven. A picture of heaven usually includes clouds, angels, and material-less existence. The Bible does not paint that picture. The Bible instructs us very clearly concerning the eternal dwelling place of those entering the kingdom of Christ. And, to the surprise of most, it includes national identities. Certain nations will continue to exist into eternity. However, determining which nations they are may be difficult. What is fascinating is that those nations will continue to exist in distinct nations for all eternity. After all, didn't YHWH say that Christ would inherit the nations (Psalm 2:8)?

The primary book to look to for this information is the book of Revelation. In that book, the writings of the Prophets, and the instructions from the Law of Moses all come to a head. It is in this magnificent book that we see what exactly will happen to the peoples of the world, and especially the nations of the world. It is important to remember that John is writing from an exclusively biblical background. The information contained in this book is built upon a proper and accurate understanding of the vast amount of instruction from the rest of the Bible, primarily the Old Testament. So, in order to understand what

John is writing, we must have a good grasp of the Old Testament Scriptures.

The sweep of the topic of nations extends from their creation in Genesis 10-11, as we have seen, to the promise of judgment in the Latter Prophets. Everything in between continues to develop the fact that the nations of the world are in a position of subjection to God, although they reject it. God's chosen nation, Israel, is the only nation on the planet who has had the true God as their God, and will remain her God into eternity (Deuteronomy 4:7-8; Revelation 21:12). To deny Israel a national presence in eternity is to undermine a majority of Scripture, as well as leave open the question, "Then what about all the other nations? Are they non-existent as well? And if so, then why are they mentioned in Revelation as present in eternity?" From the creation of the nations, we move forward to the promise of a nation to a single man married to a woman who cannot conceive. God said to Abram, "I will make you a great nation..." (Genesis 12:2). That means that from Abraham would come a family, region, and language unique to them from the descendants of this man and his wife, Sarai. Among the nations of the world, God would actively create, relate to, preserve, and establish a single nation, later to be named Israel after Abram's grandson, Jacob (Genesis 32:28). This single nation, starting as a family, would produce the Messiah who will one day, as decreed of God in Psalm 2:2, 6-7, rule from the mountain determined for Him by the Father, Mount Zion (Psalm 2:6). That mountain is none other than the location of the city of Jerusalem (Psalm 48:1-3; cp. Matthew 5:35). No other nation on the earth has God as her God.

Since it is true that the nations of the earth worship different gods, their judgment is sure to come. Historically, the nations would have been judged by God's nation, Israel, especially as it pertains to entering the land promised to them (Deuteronomy 7:1-2, 16-26). The nations worship idols. Israel is the nation of the true God, YHWH. The idols cannot save (Isaiah 46:7). YHWH is a Savior (Isaiah 45:20-23).

APPENDIX 4

SYNTACTICAL EXEGESIS OF JOHN 3:15-16

This appendix concerns itself with the more technical side of this work. I include it here for instruction, accountability, and examination. This information is not something that most people reading this book will find interesting, or helpful. However, I believe that for those that do, it is important that I include it. So, please, examine the following carefully. Where I may have been mistaken, please contact me.

The basic premise of this work has been that John 3:16 does not teach that God loves the world in the sense that He finds Himself attracted to it, or pleased with it in any way. Further, He does not love the world in the same way that He loves His Son, His Spirit, or His children. It is clear that since God is love, He does love. He does love the world and demonstrated the nature of His love historically by means of His care for it (Acts 14:16-17; Romans 1:18-21). The greatest demonstration of His love, a love primarily concerned for the Son and His kingdom, was the sending of the Son into the world. That act alone far outweighed other demonstrations of care for the world. That demonstration of love to the world was meant to produce sorrow and repentance in the world, but it did not (Romans 2:14). It actually could not. That does not make God unjust, but is simply the reality of the nature of God (absolute sovereignty) and the nature of man (absolute inability).

Contrary to modern evangelistic presentations, the gospel of Jesus Christ is the announcement that God has sent the Son into His world and as a result, the time for judgment is near (Acts 17:30-31). It is demanded of the world to repent and pay homage to the Son before He returns to judge. If you do not call upon His name, you will die in your sins. If you will call upon His name relying upon His mercy, you will be saved. The reality is, however, you will not do that, truthfully, unless the Father draws you and imparts eternal life to you of His own will, a merciful will.

In order to substantiate these things, we must include exegetical information that verifies all these findings. I will endeavor to do that below. I will present the Greek text phrase by phrase and explain what is there.

John 3:15

15 ἵνα πᾶς ὁ πιστεύων ἐν αὐτῷ ἔχῃ ζωὴν αἰώνιον.

- **ἵνα** = this particle typically, especially when used with the subjunctive mood (or mode[111]), presents a comparison to some degree of reality or fact. That is, it is either affirming a fact (thus relating to a purpose of something), or denying it. For the most part, this construction affirms a fact[112] as opposed to doubting its reality. That is to say, this particle with the subjunctive verb, ἔχῃ, provides for us an affirmation of a future reality instead of a doubtful statement as to it truthfulness. H.P.V. Nunn affirms, "(1) It is used in clauses which express the purpose of the action of the main verb. (Final clauses.). Such clauses are introduced by ἵνα or ὅπως "in order that" or "that" if affirmative, and by μή or ἵνα μή "in order that not" or "lest" if negative."[113] John's use of ἵνα with the subjunctive introduces for us the intention of the sentence. Therefore, John 3:15 is interested in telling us the intention of some action in the verse, or the surrounding context.

---

[111] Archibald T. Robertson, A *Short Grammar of the Greek New Testament, for Students Familiar With the Elements of Greek*. New York: Hodder & Stoughton, 1908), pp. 128ff.

[112] "The subjunctive glides into the realm of the future indicative on the one hand, if indeed it is not a variation of it (see Homer), and into the sphere of the imperative on the other where in fact it is supreme in the first person." *A Short Grammar*, p. 131.

[113] H. P. V. Nunn, *The Elements of New Testament Greek* (Cambridge: Cambridge University Press, 1923), 96.

- **πᾶς ὁ πιστεύων** = The construction is a singular relative pronoun + masculine singular article + masculine singular nominative, present active participle. The more exact translation would be "…every believing one…" It is the understanding that every man/person who is currently a believing one. This is a significant statement because it indicates one who is already, or at the present, a "believing one."[114] What this indicates is a man who currently demonstrates believing, and it must refer to actual believing and not false believing (see John 2:23-25). It is significant that not included in this phrase is the relative pronoun "whoever." That is most certainly not the best translation as that would include the particle combination ὃς ἄν. John is speaking here and saying that it is' the one who is a believing one' who fulfills the predicate of this verse.

- **ἐν αὐτῷ** = As Robertson notes[115], this prepositional phrase most likely modifies the verb ἔχῃ, making it "…he will possess in Him…"

---

[114] See also 3:15, 16, 18, 36; 6:35, 47; 7:38; 11:25, 26; 12:44, 46; 14:12 for the same construction with the verb πιστεύω. The construction of article plus present participle is used frequently in John (approximately 131 times).

[115] "So here ἐν αὐτῳ [en autōi] (in him) is taken with ἔχη [echēi] rather than with πιστευων [pisteuōn]." A.T. Robertson, *Word Pictures in the New Testament* (Nashville, TN: Broadman Press, 1933).

Therefore, it is only "in Him" that a man who is believing will have eternal life.

- ἔχῃ = as mentioned above, this present active subjunctive indicates, along with the ἵνα, a statement of affirmation due to purpose. That is, the purpose in mind in this verse is the possession of eternal life for those who believe and are thus "in Him." This is again affirmation of a present condition of a person and not the activity one takes part in in order to be saved. This verse, as well as v. 16 is "post-belief." That is, it is the indication that he who believes demonstrates that he possesses eternal life. This is reiterated in John 3:36 as well "He who believes in the Son *has* eternal life; but he who does not obey the Son will not see life, but the wrath of God abides on him" (emphasis mine). The possession of eternal life is just that, eternal. This life is not removed, forfeited, nor lost (John 10:28). It is these very ones who are destined not to perish and the very ones who will ever beleive. He who is believing demonstrates that he has eternal life, and will continue to have it and that is the purpose of the lifting up of the Son of Man (v. 14). The purpose of the lifting up of the Son of Man is the possession of eternal life for the believing one. This speaks to the fact that the Lord's death is meant only for those who believe and not for those who would never believe.

John 3:16

16 Οὕτως γὰρ ἠγάπησεν ὁ θεὸς τὸν κόσμον, ὥστε τὸν υἱὸν τὸν μονογενῆ ἔδωκεν, ἵνα πᾶς ὁ πιστεύων εἰς αὐτὸν μὴ ἀπόληται ἀλλ᾽ ἔχῃ ζωὴν αἰώνιον.

- **Οὕτως ἠγάπησεν** = Οὕτως indicates the manner in which something is done, or by which something exists. Although at times this indicates a sense of emphasis,[116] it is not so used here in this verse.[117] Along with the particle ὥστε, it indicates the result of the intended purpose of v. 15.[118] This particle is modifying the main verb, ἠγάπησεν. That is to say that God, being

---

[116] οὕτω Balz, Horst Robert and Gerhard Schneider. *Exegetical Dictionary of the New Testament*. Grand Rapids, Mich.: Eerdmans, 1990), p. 549.

[117] οὕτως Liddell, H.G. *A Lexicon: Abridged from Liddell and Scott's Greek-English Lexicon*. Oak Harbor, WA: Logos Research Systems, Inc., 1996. See also G. Abbott-Smith, *A Manuel Greek Lexicon of the New Testament* (Edinburgh: T&T Clark, 1921), p. 329-330.

[118] "We do not dispute that apart from ὥστε, οὕτως may indicate high degree when modifying adjectives, adverbs, and adverbial phrases; but we do wish to cast doubt on that possibility when οὕτως modifies a finite verb and occurs in combination with a ὥστε that is followed by another finite verb, as in John 3:16. Positively, we argue that in such circumstances οὕτως means "in this way" as a matter of manner other than high degree, and that in John 3:16 and numerous other texts ὥστε introduces an addition that restates or supplements something previously referenced by οὕτως." Gundry & Howell, "The Sense and Syntax...", p. 25. It must be noted that not every conclusion Dr. Gundry's article would fit the conclusions we have drawn here. However, the use of the particle in this manner, we believe, is accurate.

the subject of the verb, loved the world in some manner. This is not emphatic love, but *manner* of love; a demonstration of love. With this adverb, Jesus is telling Nicodemus that God's love was demonstrated in some manner to the world. The manner in which God demonstrated His love to the world is most readily pertaining to the Son's arrival to the earth, more than the death of the Son, as we will see. ἠγάπησεν is an aorist active indicative verb from the verb "to love." The subject of the verb is God and the direct object of the verb is the world (τὸν κόσμον-neuter, singular, accusative). This verb is the heart of the verse, as far as the verb is concerned. The aorist most regularly refers to an action at some point in time in the past, as discussed previously.[119] Thus, from the vantage point of Jesus and Nicodemus, an action in the past demonstrated the manner in which God loved the world. Obviously, that is not the crucifixion of Jesus Christ because He is speaking to Nicodemus. The incarnation is in view. However, the incarnation of the Son of God was for the purpose of dying (see John 12:27; cf. Mark 10:45). Yet, the coming of the Son into His own things is the demonstration of the love of the Father. Note also that the accusative, describing

---

[119] See J. Gresham Machen, *New Testament Greek for Beginners* (Englewood Cliffs, New Jersey: Prentice-Hall, 1923), p. 81.

the limit of the action of the verb, would typically indicate that the love of God was "for" the world. However, remember, the use of the adverb of manner is employed and that would indicate that the love is more a demonstration *to* the world. The manner of demonstration was the giving of the Son.

• τὸν υἱὸν τὸν μονογενῆ ἔδωκεν = this description of the Son is taken from Psalm 2 where the idea of the Son being "only-begotten" is used. It is a description of the Son begotten of the Father not in the incarnation, but rather in His resurrection to life from the dead. ἔδωκεν, an aorist active indicative, indicates that God "gave" the Son to the world, into the world, as a demonstration of His love. This is a very extensive love. Again, the aorist would indicate an the action of giving at a point in time in the past. This is not the direct reference to the giving of the Son on the cross, as that is yet future to Jesus, the Speaker.[120] However, the giving of the Son most indicates His birth. The picture is painted by the Lord clearly in Matthew 21:33-44, the parable of the landowner.

---

[120] Contra Robertson, *Word Pictures*, John 3:15.

- ἵνα πᾶς ὁ πιστεύων εἰς αὐτὸν = again, another explanatory particle that introduces the clause following as an explanation for the giving of the Son, which itself is a demonstration of the love of God. "In order that" indicates purpose or resolution and the purpose involves "every believing one/man" (πᾶς ὁ πιστεύων) in some way. The use of the typical Johannine participle + εἰς + direct object is here, as opposed to the previous verse which uses ἐν, indicating that ἐν most properly belongs with ἔχῃ. Notice that the subject of the intention is not the world. Whatever the giving of the Son as a demonstration of love *to* the world is, it is for the purpose of something to do with the "one (who is) a believing one." The limits of the giving of the Son are strictly here demonstrated.

- μὴ ἀπόληται ἀλλ᾽ ἔχῃ ζωὴν αἰώνιον = Once again, John introduces the subjunctive with the explanatory conjunction above. The statement of affirmation and purpose, as discussed above, is that the one believing "would not perish." According to John 10:26-28, only those who are the sheep of Jesus Christ, those given from the Father to the Son (John 6:35-40; 17:2, 24), will believe. The goats will never believe. They are the tares, the sons of the evil one (Matthew 13:38; cf. 1 John 3:7-10) are not to be redeemed. However, those who are categorized as "he who is a believing one" will never perish and that is the mission of the Lord Jesus Christ (Matthew 10:5-6; 15:24; Luke 15). It is a repeated theme in John that those who are "believing ones" would not perish (6:39; 10:10, 28; 17:12; 18:9). Thus, the Lord's ministry is properly summed up as a rescue mission for the sheep of God, those who would believe, those who are not to perish, as much as Satan has attempted to guarantee their death (Genesis 3:1-5; cf. Hebrews 2:14; 1 John 3:8).

- ἀλλ' ἔχη ζωὴν αἰώνιον = in contrast to perishing, the coming of the Son, as a demonstration of love to the world, God determined that the children of God would not perish but rather "possess" eternal life. With this statement, we see the ultimate intention, purpose, of God in the sending of the Son. His purpose, indicated again by the repeated subjunctive in conjunction with the previous subjunctive and ἵνα, is to give eternal life to the "believing ones," the 'πᾶς ὁ πιστεύων.' This limits

His intentions to the ones whom He gave to the Son, who are the only ones who will ever believe (John 10:25-30). Only those whom the Father has created to give to the Son will ever believe and only they will receive eternal life.

211

Subject

Index

Scripture Index

Genesis

Psalms

Proverbs

Ecclesiastes

Isaiah

Jeremiah

Ezekiel

Daniel

Hosea

Matthew

Mark

Luke

John

Acts

Romans

BIBLIOGRAPHY

Abbott-Smith, G. *A Manuel Greek Lexicon of the New Testament.* Edingburgh: T&T Clark, 1921.

Bainton, Roland. *The Church of Our Fathers.* Salem: Schmul, 1987.

Balz, Horst Robert, and Gerhard Schieder. *Exegetical Dictionary of the New Testament.* Grand Rapids: Eerdmans, 1990.

Balz, Horst Robert, and Gerhard Schneider. *Exegetical Dictionary of the New Testament.* Grand Rapids: Eerdmans, 1990.

Borchert, Gerald L. *New American Commentary: John 1-11.* Vol. 25A. Nashville: Broadman, 1996.

Calvin, John. *John.* Edited by Alister McGrath, & J.I. Packer. Wheaton: Crossway, 1994.

Cole, R. Dennis. *Numbers: The New American Commentary.* Nashville: Broadmane & Holman, 2000.

Daiches, Rabbie Dr. Samuel , Rev. Dr. Israel W. Slotki, and Rabbi Dr. I. Epstein. *Soncino Babylonian Talmud.* Edited by Rabbi Dr. I. Epstein. London, n.d.

Demarest, Bruce. *The Cross and Salvation.* Wheaton: Crossway, 1997.

Edersheim, Alfred. *The Temple, Its Ministry and Services As They Were at the Time of Jesus Christ.* Bellingham, Wa: Logos Bible Software, 2003.

Friberg, Timothy, Barbara Friberg, and Miller F. Neva. *Analytical Lexicon of the Greek New Testament.* Grand Rapids: Baker, 2000.

Grudem, Wayne. *Systematic Theology.* Grand Rapids: Zondervan, 1994.

Gundry, Robert, and Russell Howell. "THE SENSE AND SYNTAX OF JOHN 3:14-17 WITH SPECIAL REFERENCE TO THE USE OF "ΟΥΤΩΣ ... "ΩΣΤΕ IN JOHN 3:16." *Novum Testamentum* 41, no. 1 (January 1999): 24-39.

Keil, Carl Freidrich, and Franz Delitzsch. *Commentary On The Old Testament.* Peabody, MA: Hendrickson Publishers Incoporated, 1996.

Kiline, Meredith. "Two Adams, Two Covenants of Works." *The Upper Register.* 2007. www.upper-register.com (accessed January 6, 2014).

Kittel, Gerhard, Gerhard Friedrich, and Geoffrey Bromiley. *Theological Dictionary of the New Testament.* Grand Rapids, 1964.

Liddell, H.G. *A Lexicon: Abridged From Liddell and Scott's Greek-English Lexicon.* Oak Harbor: Logos Research Systems, 1996.

MacArthur, John. *The Love of God: He Will Do Whatever It Takes To Make Us Holy.* Dallas: Word Publishing, 1996.

Machen, J. Gresham. *New Testament Greek for Beginners.* Englewood Cliffs, New Jersey: Prentice-Hall, 1923.

McMahon, C. Matthew. *A Puritan's Mind.* n.d. http://www.apuritansmind.com/arminianism/an-exegetical-look-at-john-316-by-dr-c-matthew-mcmahon/ (accessed January 14, 2014).

Nunn, H.P.V. *The Elements of New Testament Greek.* Cambridge: Cambridge University Press, 1923.

Robert B. Chisholm, Jr. *From Exegesis To Exposition.* Grand Rapids: Baker, 1998.

Robertson, A.T. *A Grammar of the Greek New Testament.* Nashville: Broadman, 1934.

Robertson, Archibald T. *A Short Grammar of the Greek New Testament, for Student Familiar With the Elements of Greek.* New York: Hodder and Stoughton, 1908.

—. *Word Pictures in the New Testament .* Nashville: Broadman Press, 1933.

Witsius, Hermann. *The Economy of the Covenants Between God and Man.* London: Thomas Nelson, 1822.

www.ingramcontent.com/pod-product-compliance
Lightning Source LLC
LaVergne TN
LVHW051504080426
835509LV00017B/1909